THE VERY
BRITISH
PROBLEMS

QUIZ BOOK

THE VERY BRITISH PROBLEMS

QUIZ BOOK

Rob Temple

SPHERE

SPHERE

First published in Great Britain in 2022 by Sphere

3 5 7 9 10 8 6 4 2

A CIP catalogue record for this book
is available from the British Library.

ISBN 978-0-7515-8534-6

Typeset in Caslon by M Rules
Printed and bound in Great Britain by
Clays Ltd, Elcograf S.p.A.

Papers used by Sphere are from well-managed forests
and other responsible sources.

MIX
Paper from
responsible sources
FSC® C104740

Sphere
An imprint of
Little, Brown Book Group
Carmelite House
50 Victoria Embankment
London EC4Y 0DZ

An Hachette UK Company
www.hachette.co.uk

www.littlebrown.co.uk

For Sumin

CONTENTS

INTRODUCTION

Hello! Long time no see. Come in, come in. You look well. How are you? If you just replied to that question in any way, congratulations – you just answered the very first question of many in this official Very British Problems quiz book! It's been a decade since I started highlighting the oddities of the nation (see @SoVeryBritish on Twitter for proof!) and, if you don't mind me saying, we as a people are still just as weird as ever. Very British Problems now has over five million followers over all social media, as well as lots of books, which tells me it's probably struck a chord.

Anyway, where was I? Yes! If pubs and teatime television have taught us anything, it's that we all love a good quiz, don't we? So with that in mind I've written a book of questions on all things British (plus a chapter or two on the rest of the world, just for balance).

Inside this testing tome you'll find queues of questions lined up patiently on every page, on all sorts of Very British topics, that will keep you scratching your head until it's just a pile of dandruffy dust.

Serving suggestions: You could use this book to have raucous but studious fun with friends. Or enjoy it around the dinner table with family. Or take it to the pub quiz you run and claim you wrote it all yourself. Or, let's think ... you could use it to prop up that wobbly leg on the bedside table. Though, if you ask me (thanks for asking me, nobody ever asks me anything) it's probably best enjoyed, like most things in life, all alone in a cold conservatory on a rainy day with a pot of tea on the side.

Right, must get on. Take care, see you soon, all best, cheerio, bye bye bye. Bye. Oh, hang on, before I go, I meant to say, you can find all the answers in the back! I'd forget my own head if it wasn't screwed on. Right, keys, wallet, phone, think that's everything ... right, bye! Bye bye bye.

Rob Temple, Cambridge

WEATHER

We're obsessed with the weather (what's it doing now? Chucking it down, is it? Oh gosh, I think the washing's out! Nooooo!) but how much do we actually know about it? Well, let's find out.

(All answers correct at time of writing, i.e. early 2022.)

Q1.

Where is the least snowy place in Britain?

    a)   Cornwall
    b)   Oxford
    c)   Durham

Q2.

In his famous poem, what did William Wordsworth wander lonely as?

    a)   A breeze
    b)   A cloud
    c)   A puddle

Q3.

Which nation recorded the lowest minimum UK temperature in 1982, according to Met Office data?

a) England
b) Northern Ireland
c) Scotland

Q4.

What was that lowest minimum temperature mentioned in question 3?

a) -7.2°C
b) -17.2°C
c) -27.2°C

Q5.

What sort of weather condition is usually associated with a phrase mentioning cats and dogs?

a) Rain
b) Wind
c) Fog

Q6.

What type of weather accessory does Mary Poppins use to help her fly?

a) Sunglasses
b) A waterproof coat
c) An umbrella

Q7.

The naming system of what weather phenomenon never includes names related to the British Royal Family, nor the letters Q, U, X, Y or Z?

a) Storms
b) Heatwaves
c) Tidal waves

Q8.

According to a 2015 Very British Problems (@SoVeryBritish) poll, which season do Brits love the most?

a) Spring
b) Summer
c) Autumn

Q9.

According to the University of Westminster, 80,000 of which weather-related item are left on the London Underground each year?

a) Raincoats
b) Sun hats
c) Umbrellas

Q10.

Where is the soggiest city in Britain, so says the Met Office?

a) Manchester
b) Cardiff
c) Glasgow

Q11.

What type of weather is associated with a phrase meaning 'to have a large amount of work to do'?

a) Snow
b) Hail
c) Sleet

Q12.

When was the last time the River Thames completely froze over?

    a) 1892
    b) 1921
    c) 1963

Q13.

At the climax of the 1994 British film *Four Weddings and a Funeral*, what type of weather does Andie MacDowell's character, Carrie, famously not notice?

    a) Rain
    b) Gale-force winds
    c) Fog

Q14.

Which month is synonymous with 'showers'?

    a) March
    b) April
    c) May

Q15.

In June 1975, several county cricket matches had to be abandoned due to what type of weather?

a) Too much heat
b) Too much wind
c) Too much snow

Q16.

Gather round, cloud spotters. According to the BBC's *Cloud Spotting Guide*, what is the most common type of cloud in the UK?

a) Stratocumulus
b) Cirrus
c) Nimbostratus

Q17.

In which recent year did the UK have the wettest February on record?

a) 2019
b) 2020
c) 2021

Q18.

What is British weather actually for?

- a) It's a mystery but I wish it would just behave itself.
- b) Sometimes the garden needs it.
- c) To give us something easy to talk about if we bump into the neighbours.

Q19.

Which of these names belongs to one of the most famous weather forecasters in British television history?

- a) Matthew Cod
- b) Michael Fish
- c) Mark Guppy

Q20.

And why is the weather forecaster from question 19 particularly notable?

- a) He correctly predicted the exact amount of rainfall every day for a week.
- b) He said a hurricane definitely wasn't on the way shortly before the worst storm to hit southeast England in three centuries.
- c) He presented the weather every single day for a decade.

Q21.

What usually gets blown onto the railway tracks to cause travel disruptions on British trainlines?

a) Swans
b) Litter
c) Leaves

Q22.

Which of these is the name of a famous Scottish rock band – perhaps most famous for their recording of the hit song, 'Love is all Around' – that most accurately describes a British day?

a) Wet Wet Wet
b) Hot Hot Hot
c) Brisk Brisk Brisk

Q23.

An anemometer is used to measure what?

a) Rainfall
b) Wind speed
c) Heatwaves

Q24.

In Ruthin in North Wales in 1947, the deepest snow in an inhabited area of the UK was recorded. How deep was it, according to the Met Office?

    a)   1.65 metres
    b)   4.65 metres
    c)   7.65 metres

Q25.

How many British phrases exist to describe how rain is coming down?

    a)   10
    b)   50
    c)   Limitless

Q26.

When it gets really hot in Britain, what do people most commonly claim you could fry on the pavement?

    a)   Pancakes
    b)   An egg
    c)   Bubble and squeak

Q27.

'It's raining, it's pouring, the old man is . . .' what?

    a)   Boring

    b)   Snoring

    c)   Laying down some new flooring

Q28.

What weather condition's name is derived from the Norse god Thor?

    a)   Tornados

    b)   Giant hail

    c)   Thunder

Q29.

What was the nationality of inventor Charles Macintosh, whom the Mackintosh (with added letter k!) is named after?

    a)   English

    b)   Welsh

    c)   Scottish

Q30.

What type of coat is marmalade-loving bear Paddington famous for wearing?

a) Waterproof cagoule
b) Duffel coat
c) Trench coat

Q31.

When was The Great Smog of London?

a) 1752
b) 1852
c) 1952

WEATHER DEFENDERS

Find the ten pieces of armour Brits wear to conquer four seasons in one day.

```
W  H  B  G  C  S  E  S  S  A  L  G  N  U  S
C  S  S  S  Z  H  F  H  U  K  O  N  I  Y  R
V  J  P  O  E  B  L  A  A  Z  A  O  R  K  E
W  Q  U  A  T  E  O  R  T  G  S  Y  E  Y  P
B  X  Y  Z  P  N  O  L  I  R  N  C  I  T  P
F  A  U  R  R  N  I  D  E  W  E  I  A  Z  I
Z  M  L  J  A  J  R  K  P  Q  T  T  K  R  L
F  O  G  A  H  A  Z  A  C  H  T  Q  N  U  F
T  Z  M  R  C  K  L  A  F  A  I  U  P  K  S
S  J  T  I  W  L  K  Q  X  O  M  E  Y  N  S
S  D  T  Y  E  V  A  H  U  U  A  X  A  I  Q
B  I  D  R  Y  X  F  V  J  W  U  Q  L  W  N
Y  O  B  N  T  M  M  A  A  J  K  B  Q  B  B
E  M  W  E  L  L  I  E  S  I  E  S  E  I  Z
U  U  K  B  T  O  O  M  Q  P  S  J  G  W  A
```

Anorak	Mackintosh	Umbrella
Balaclava	Mittens	Wellies
Cardigan	Scarf	
Flippers	Sunglasses	

COCKNEY RHYMING SLANG

A quiz for those born within earshot of Bow Bells. Just read the rhyming slang and decide what the ding dong bell it's meant to mean, guv'nor.

Rhyming slang, whereby words in phrases are changed to make the original meaning elusive to those not in the know (especially handy if you're a criminal standing next to an eavesdropping policeman), originated in East London in the early nineteenth century, leading to Australian and American versions becoming popular in their own right.

Q1.
'Apples and pears'

- a) Bears
- b) Tupperwares
- c) Stairs

Q2.
'Box of toys'

- a) Noise
- b) Boys
- c) Football manager David Moyes

Q3.
'Didn't ought'

- a) Port
- b) Sort
- c) Abort

Q4.
'Early hours'

- a) Towers
- b) Flowers
- c) Austin Powers

Q5.
'Duck and dive'

- a) Survive
- b) Thrive
- c) Hide

Q6.
'Lump of ice'

- a) Advice
- b) Twice
- c) Mice

Q7.
'Pleasure and pain'

    a)   Stain

    b)   Rain

    c)   A very clever brain

Q8.
'Weep and wail'

    a)   Fail

    b)   Royal Mail

    c)   A tale

Q9.
'Whistle and flute'

    a)   Suit

    b)   Boot

    c)   Beetroot

Q10.
'Treacle tart'

    a)   Shopping cart

    b)   Sweetheart

    c)   Priceless art

Q11.

'Ruby Murray'

    a)   Curry

    b)   Hurry

    c)   A very sunburnt tennis player

Q12.

'Kettle and hob'

    a)   Doorknob

    b)   Rob (as in 'to steal')

    c)   A watch

Q13.

'Barnet Fair'

    a)   Double dare

    b)   Hair

    c)   The Fresh Prince of Bel Air

Q14.

'Custard and jelly'

    a)   Telly

    b)   Welly

    c)   Deli

Q15.

'Borrow and beg'

- a) Egg
- b) Gregg
- c) Leg

Q16.

'Crowded space'

- a) Slap in the face
- b) A large waist
- c) Suitcase

Q17.

'Pig and roast'

- a) Post
- b) Toast
- c) Ghost

Q18.

'Rats and mice'

- a) Five spice
- b) Paradise
- c) Dice

Q19.

'Adam and Eve'

- a) Believe
- b) Some bloke named Steve
- c) Get up and leave

Q20.

'Jack Jones'

- a) Alone
- b) Loans
- c) Moans and groans

Q21.

'Barney Rubble'

- a) Stubble
- b) Double
- c) Trouble

Q22.

'Boat race'

- a) Briefcase
- b) Face
- c) Absolute disgrace

Q23.
'Hampstead Heath'

- a) Roast beef
- b) Underneath
- c) Teeth

Q24.
'Tea leaf'

- a) Thief
- b) Chief
- c) Richards, Keith

Q25.
'Scooby-Doo'

- a) Loo
- b) Chew
- c) Clue

Q26.
'Aunt Joanna'

- a) Piano
- b) Banana
- c) Americana

Q27.

'Butcher's hook'

- a) Ration book
- b) Meat cook
- c) Look

Q28.

'Almond rocks'

- a) Clocks
- b) Socks
- c) Docks

Q29.

'Battlecruiser'

- a) Loser
- b) Boozer
- c) Boxer/fighter

Q30.

'Bees and honey'

- a) Sunny
- b) Funny
- c) Money

FOOD AND DRINK

Boil the kettle, make yourself a cup of something warm (as long as it's tea) and crack open the Hobnobs to nourish your brain for these tasty teasers.

Q1.

Which of the following is a type of chicken dish, usually yellow in colour with the predominant flavouring of curry powder?

  a) Coronation Chicken
  b) Eastenders Chicken
  c) Emmerdale Chicken

Q2.

According to a Very British Problems (@SoVeryBritish) poll, which sauce most belongs on a bacon sandwich?

Q3.

In what month in Britain is National Yorkshire Pudding Day celebrated?

Q4.

What should you do with the last roast potato?

a) Leave it to go in the bin, it's gone cold anyway and it's only a cooked potato.
b) Wrap it in cling film and put it in the fridge until later.
c) Offer it to everyone, hope everybody says no and then eat it yourself with any remaining gravy.

Q5.

A 'Snowball' is a retro cocktail, traditionally enjoyed at Christmas in Britain, containing which alcoholic beverage?

a) Crème de menthe
b) Advocaat
c) Absinthe

Q6.

What sort of sweet is also the name of something shouted by Charles Dickens' character Ebenezer Scrooge, when he dislikes something that's generally seen as enjoyable?

a) Bah! Toffee!
b) Bah! Humbug!
c) Bah! Mint Imperial!

Q7.

According to a Very British Problems (@SoVeryBritish) poll, which meat is the nation's favourite when it comes to a Sunday roast dinner?

- a) Chicken
- b) Pork
- c) Beef
- d) Lamb

Q8.

According to the UK Tea & Infusions Association, how many cups of tea do Brits drink each year?

- a) 60.2 million
- b) 60.2 billion
- c) 60.2 trillion

Q9.

Which brand of tea would you associate with chimps and the character 'Monkey'?

- a) Twinings
- b) Tetley
- c) PG Tips

Q10.

What is the optimum boiling time for Brussels sprouts?

    a)   5 minutes

    b)   5 hours

    c)   5 days

Q11.

Which restaurant chain opened its first UK branch in Woolwich, south London, in October 1974?

    a)   McDonald's

    b)   Burger King

    c)   Wimpy

Q12.

What was the name of the television show that first turned Jamie Oliver into a household name? It first aired in 1999.

    a)   *The Nude Cook*

    b)   *The Naked Chef*

    c)   *The Baker in the Buff*

Q13.

Which British soul band had a hit in 1975 with the song 'You Sexy Thing'?

a) Hot Coffee
b) Hot Chocolate
c) Hot Toddy

Q14.

According to a Perspectus Global poll in 2020, which flavour of Walkers Crisps was named Britain's favourite?

a) Smoky Bacon
b) Ready Salted
c) Cheese & Onion

Q15.

What type of meaty product would you expect to see hiding inside a Yorkshire pudding in the dish Toad in the Hole?

a) Sausages
b) Fillet steak
c) Meatballs

Q16.

Traditionally, the British asparagus season runs from St George's Day on 23 April to what special day?

 a) Father's Day
 b) St Swithun's Day
 c) Summer solstice

Q17.

Which British band topped the UK charts in late 1968 with a cover of The Beatles song, 'Ob-La-Di, Ob-La-Da'?

 a) Marmalade
 b) The Jam
 c) Cream

Q18.

Bisto (you know, the gravy) is an acronym for:

 a) Browns Instantly, Seasons and Thickens in One
 b) Bastes, Improves Sausages, Tasty and Odourless
 c) Best Indulgent Seasoning, Terrifically Opulent

Q19.

Who was on the throne when Marmite was created?

Q20.

Where in Wales does Tintern cheese originate?

a) Carmarthenshire
b) Monmouthshire
c) Pembrokeshire

Q21.

What is the most popular type of milk in the UK according to Statista.com?

a) Skimmed
b) Semi-skimmed
c) Whole

Q22.

The instruction to 'have a break' is linked to the subsequent enjoyment of which popular chocolate snack?

a) Twix
b) Mars Bar
c) KitKat

Q23.

What is the most popular pub name in the UK? A packet of pork scratchings for you if you get it right.

Q24.

Complete the title of the 1961 Roald Dahl book: *James and the Giant...?*

Q25.

Where did the Great Fire of London start in 1666?

    a) Pudding Lane
    b) Bread Street
    c) Baker's Row

Q26.

What fruit sits atop the singles trophy presented to the winner of the gentlemen's final at Wimbledon?

    a) Pineapple
    b) Apple
    c) Banana

Q27.
When making a cup of tea, does the milk go in first or last?

Q28.
A barm cake is a ... what?

Q29.
What food is traditionally 'piped' into the room during supper on Burns Night?

Q30.
On what street in London would you find 'Rules', London's oldest restaurant?

a) Brick Lane
b) Maiden Lane
c) Bear Lane

ROAST DINNER

Here you'll find hidden ten of the foods and condiments that make up a Sunday roast. Warning: some may be controversial and cause arguments.

M	V	E	E	Z	U	O	C	H	L	I	K	E	O	C
H	V	D	S	R	Y	V	A	R	G	P	C	J	A	F
V	S	V	A	Y	S	Q	R	E	C	U	C	U	U	Y
E	I	I	Q	N	O	L	R	O	A	V	L	Q	O	W
G	I	A	D	W	I	H	O	S	A	I	Y	R	I	O
A	W	Y	V	A	A	Y	T	V	F	S	K	X	L	L
N	P	G	X	U	R	N	S	L	V	S	T	H	L	K
O	G	R	O	L	I	E	O	Z	H	C	W	I	Q	V
P	G	B	A	M	E	W	S	I	L	I	K	Q	E	H
T	E	M	M	I	E	A	R	R	D	B	S	U	M	S
I	N	A	V	R	I	E	Y	W	O	P	R	M	F	A
O	A	L	A	F	S	Y	C	M	V	H	H	Z	F	K
N	K	R	N	G	W	D	P	A	R	S	N	I	P	S
P	Y	M	E	M	D	H	B	U	W	V	A	E	Z	E
S	I	L	T	J	D	Q	H	D	F	K	W	C	C	E

Carrots   Lamb   Vegan option
Cauliflower   Mint sauce   Yorkshires
Gravy   Parsnips
Horseradish   Roasties

PIECE OF CAKE

Find all ten types of cake hidden here and then treat yourself to one of them!

```
I  V  Q  Q  E  Q  Z  T  P  E  B  E  G  R  E
Y  G  V  N  F  K  N  X  S  L  I  K  X  E  G
T  O  R  R  A  C  A  I  A  M  S  A  T  D  N
D  L  O  G  L  I  O  C  Y  I  V  C  C  V  O
X  B  E  L  D  N  K  K  E  Q  W  P  K  E  P
T  A  E  M  E  F  T  J  W  S  I  U  H  L  S
J  I  L  G  O  R  P  O  K  T  E  C  O  V  A
O  Q  E  R  V  N  F  R  I  U  H  E  U  E  I
S  D  E  F  Y  D  D  R  B  I  T  O  H  T  R
F  S  J  A  F  F  A  R  V  T  Z  K  P  C  O
T  L  V  U  F  M  B  K  I  Z  S  P  G  H  T
U  R  L  W  I  K  B  N  D  Z  W  W  L  L  C
A  U  L  S  P  U  Y  R  F  K  Z  F  Q  D  I
M  T  U  Z  U  D  P  N  N  B  C  L  N  G  V
N  D  W  J  T  O  N  Z  D  W  P  D  E  G  B
```

Black Forest	Genoise	Tiramisu
Carrot	Jaffa	Victoria sponge
Cheesecake	Lemon drizzle	
Cupcake	Red velvet	

BRITISH EVENTS

Get your shoes on, pack a brolly and a cagoule: we're going out! We're not really, thank God. Sit down again. What we're doing is trying to answer these questions about the British calendar year.

Q1.

Nice easy one to start. On what night do coat-wearing Brits huddle together in parks to watch the effigy of a man being burned to bits on top of a bonfire?

Q2.

Which of the four UK patron saints' days comes first in the year?

Q3.

On what day are you most likely to see in the news that scientists have learned how to grow spaghetti from a tree and/or a farmer has bred the world's first flying pig?

Q4.

In what month would you celebrate (or be informed about via that friend on social media who's really into witches) the summer solstice?

Q5.

What London street party has been held every August bank holiday since the mid-1960s?

Q6.

In what month is a usually shaved-upper-lipped Brit most likely to grow a moustache in support of men's health?

Q7.

On what day are you most likely to eat turkey?

Q8.

To the nearest million, how many cards (according to research by Finder.com) are sent in Britain each year for Valentine's Day?

Q9.

In which British county does the Glastonbury Festival take place?

Q10.

What simple meal might you find yourself eating forty-seven days before Easter Sunday?

Q11.

What summer event is also known as the 'Queen's Birthday Parade'?

Q12.

What type of cheese (a large wheel of it) is chased down a hill at the Cooper's Hill Cheese-Rolling and Wake annual spring event?

Q13.

What is the name of the Monday in January that marks the traditional start of the English agricultural year? It's named after a farming tool.

Q14.

During what event, originating in medieval times, would you encounter Tutti Men on Tutti Day?

Q15.

What square in London hosts Europe's largest outdoor Diwali celebration each year?

Q16.

The World _____ Eating Championship takes place at The Bottle Inn in Dorset each year. Fill in the blank (clue: it's a particularly painful type of salad).

Q17.

The first Monday in which month has become known as National Sickie Day, which is said to be the day when most Brits take a day off work for illness (or just to get some lovely sofa time)?

Q18.

In what year was the Queen's Golden Jubilee?

Q19.

Over how many days does Hogmanay take place? Is it one, two, three or four?

Q20.

True or false: The Chelsea Flower Show was formerly known as the Beautiful Bloomers Show.

Q21.

Where would you most likely see a Rhodesian Ridgeback – at Crufts, at London Fashion Week or at the Taste of London Food Festival?

Q22.

J. S. Fry & Sons, better known as Fry's, introduced the first chocolate what in Britain?

Q23.

In what month does the Edinburgh Fringe Festival take place?

Q24.

On what birthday might you expect to receive a letter of congratulations from Buckingham Palace?

Q25.

The Straw Bear Festival takes place in which English county?

Q26.

Which bird gives its name to the famous annual travelling funfair held in Nottingham?

Q27.

Shakespeare's birthday is celebrated in Stratford-upon-Avon in which month?

Q28.

On what river would you take part in the annual ceremony of 'swan upping'?

Q29.

In what month is BBC *Children in Need* broadcast?

Q30.

Which of these is NOT in the lyrics to 'Auld Lang Syne', traditionally sung at the start of the New Year: 'We'll tak a right gude-willy waught' or 'We'll tak a wrong bad-wangly caught'?

VERY BRITISH MUSIC FESTIVALS

Complete this round while hung over in a tent for maximum realism.

ACROSS

4. The UK's most prestigious electronic dance music festival (11)
8. This Rebel Rebel headlined Glastonbury in the year 2000 (5, 5)
9. London location of the BST (or British Summer Time) festival (4, 4)
10. Surname of the English dairy farmer who co-created Glasto (5)

DOWN

1. A festival that's an antonym of longitude (8)

2. Festival veterans whose albums include *Parachutes* and *X&Y* (8)
3. A pair of simultaneously showcased annual festivals, one in Leeds and the other in … (7)
5. British music festival known as 'the Woodstock of Europe' (4, 2, 5)
6. Somerset village, home to the Glastonbury Festival (6)
7. Perhaps the most famous triangular stage of all UK music festivals (7)

BRITISH BANDS

Find ten bands from Britain to have rocked it all over the world (that may be a clue to one of them).

```
L  B  N  X  A  S  X  T  Q  D  N  X  W  P  S
N  L  G  O  I  X  A  U  U  Q  C  I  S  I  T
G  U  E  S  I  K  M  R  X  X  U  M  W  S  A
V  R  A  Q  E  S  A  M  H  C  W  E  G  J  T
W  O  P  T  N  N  I  P  C  K  N  L  E  E  U
Y  G  H  M  D  H  B  V  P  M  H  T  Q  N  S
U  A  T  U  T  Y  H  U  I  V  N  T  X  F  Q
T  E  R  O  L  E  I  H  S  D  R  I  K  C  U
F  A  S  I  S  E  N  E  G  O  Y  L  F  K  O
N  P  I  N  K  F  L  O  Y  D  V  O  H  H  C
M  P  U  W  N  S  R  I  V  T  E  A  J  P  U
V  Y  P  Q  S  T  Z  O  H  E  G  F  M  X  P
W  O  P  K  M  R  P  M  S  C  Z  Y  U  T  P
J  A  C  I  R  T  E  R  X  M  Z  R  U  M  C
I  L  G  P  Z  G  J  U  T  Y  P  Q  H  Y  O
```

Blur	Little Mix	Status Quo
Duran Duran	Oasis	Take That
Genesis	Pink Floyd	
Joy Division	Queen	

BRITISH SPORTS

Put on your boots, tie up your laces, strap on your helmets, saddle up, rev your engines and get ready for the whistle ... and ... GO GO GO! Yes, it's the very British sports quiz. Howzat!

Q1.
The men's Boat Race takes place annually between Cambridge and Oxford. Which team has won the most races to date?

Q2.
In 1877, the only what was recorded in Boat Race history?

Q3.
Which famous British race passes the *Cutty Sark* at mile 6?

Q4.

Who 'parachuted' into the opening ceremony of the
London 2012 Olympics, accompanied by James Bond?

Q5.

Which of these is a real sporting event: bog snorkelling
or swamp cycling?

Q6.

Which two teams went head to head in what is officially
recognised by FIFA as football's first-ever international
match?

Q7.

Which of the open tournaments did British tennis player
Emma Raducanu win (becoming the youngest British
person to do so) in 2021 – was it the Australian Open,
the French Open, Wimbledon or the US Open?

Q8.

Which British football team has the nickname 'The
Posh'?

Q9.

What type of animal would you expect to see competing annually at Burghley House near Stamford, Lincolnshire?

Q10.

In which country did Sir Lewis Hamilton secure his first Grand Prix win in 2007 at the age of 22?

Q11.

Which Brit was the first winner of the European Footballer of the Year award in 1956?

Q12.

On what day of the week did Jessica Ennis-Hill, Greg Rutherford and Mo Farah all win gold within 44 minutes inside the Olympic stadium in 2012?

Q13.

Which Brit was the first person in the world to run under the four-minute mile?

Q14.

Who is England's all-time top wicket-taker, the only fast bowler to have taken over 600 Test wickets?

Q15.

Where is the World Darts Championship held every year?

Q16.

Who is the Wales national rugby team's most-capped player?

Q17.

In what game must Chasers or Keepers try to get the Quaffle?

Q18.

Thanks to a drop goal from Jonny Wilkinson, England won against Australia to secure the 2003 Rugby World Cup. How many points did England score?

Q19.

What type of vehicle has been raced in the Isle of Man TT races, considered one of the most dangerous races in the world, since 1907?

Q20.

True or false: Gary Lineker never received a single yellow card in his sixteen-year playing career.

Q21.

'I wouldn't say I was the best manager in the business, but I was in the top one' is a famous quote from which iconic British football manager?

Q22.

Brit Phil Shaw is famous for popularising which sport: Extreme Ironing, Danger Vacuuming or Mountain Fridge Walking?

Q23.

Paula Radcliffe won the BBC Sports Personality of the Year award in which year in the noughties?

Q24.

Which British football team has the nickname 'The Toffees'?

Q25.

The British Heart Foundation London to Brighton Bike Ride is how many miles?

Q26.

How many balls, including the white, are on a snooker table at the start of the frame? You must answer within ten seconds.

Q27.

How many gold medals did Great Britain win in the Tokyo 2020 Paralympic Games?

    a) 21
    b) 31
    c) 41

Q28.

What is the name of the horse that won the Grand National three times – the only horse to date with that claim to fame?

Q29.

Which British boxer was born in Lambeth in 1934, and remains the only boxer to ever receive a knighthood?

Q30.

In which Scottish city would you find rival football fans from Hearts and Hibs?

Q31.

If you were competing in a velodrome, what would you most likely be sat on?

WHO SAID IT?

Match the quote to the famous Brit

*'It is a well-known fact that ninety per cent
of all foreign tourists come from abroad.'*

*'Now this is not the end. It is not even the beginning
of the end. But it is, perhaps, the end of the beginning.'*

'Reality leaves a lot to the imagination.'

*'Jogging is for people who aren't intelligent
enough to watch television.'*

*'Let us not take ourselves too seriously. None
of us has a monopoly on wisdom.'*

Winston Churchill

Victoria Wood

Queen Elizabeth II

Del Boy

John Lennon

PRIME MINISTERS

Hidden here are ten of the Prime Ministers who have led Britain. Whether they led Britain to glory or not is up for debate.

```
C  M  T  S  B  E  I  N  R  V  A  U  T  G  N
Z  Z  A  R  P  A  K  E  M  U  T  T  H  N  I
W  L  O  Y  F  R  N  N  Z  J  T  L  A  K  A
Z  W  N  O  R  E  M  A  C  C  L  B  T  H  L
N  S  S  E  G  W  L  S  H  I  E  Q  C  V  R
X  O  Y  D  I  E  A  P  H  G  E  I  H  O  E
X  F  Y  L  J  E  K  C  I  T  A  X  E  K  B
I  P  S  N  M  J  R  P  N  F  A  L  R  Y  M
D  O  B  W  U  U  B  D  G  D  R  C  L  P  A
N  L  Y  L  H  E  O  M  R  A  Q  T  T  A  H
W  O  V  C  G  L  A  D  S  T  O  N  E  I  C
C  V  R  M  I  V  D  Y  J  X  P  B  N  Z  M
P  V  S  N  S  D  I  O  E  X  F  X  X  R  J
K  V  P  Y  E  U  H  I  A  C  A  Q  S  W  W
B  H  A  T  G  T  X  V  G  E  H  X  Y  Q  G
```

Attlee	Chamberlain	Thatcher
Brown	Churchill	Wilson
Callaghan	Gladstone	
Cameron	May	

STRANGE HISTORICAL HAPPENINGS

A LOT of uncommon and odd stuff has happened in Britain over the years, some of which is detailed in this round. Also in this round are a lot of the odd things that didn't happen at all! Fun and mysterious, isn't it? Essentially, I'm saying this is a true or false round. Good luck!

Q1.

In 1814 in London, a gigantic vat exploded at a brewery, releasing a huge wave of beer into the streets. It's known as the London Beer Flood.

Q2.

Llanfairpwllgwyngyllgogerychwyrndrobwllllantysilio gogogoch (fifty-eight letters!) in Wales is the longest one-word place name in the world. The use of this long name is said to have been first introduced in the nineteenth century to develop commercial and tourist interests in the area.

Q3.

The largest simultaneous roast dinner, including 280kg of beef and 200kg of carrots, is a Guinness World Record achieved by 1,632 people in Peterborough. They had apple crumble for dessert.

Q4.

In 2014, David Buzzman left an umbrella on Mars. Although he didn't personally stand on the surface, the British NASA scientist instructed the Mars Rover to hide the brolly under a rock on his behalf.

Q5.

In the 1400s, King James II of Scotland outlawed golf.

Q6.

The London Necropolis Railway was a railway line made specifically to carry corpses out of London to a cemetery in Surrey. It ran from 1854 for eighty-seven years.

07.

In 2001, the floors of certain tube stations in London were covered in a specially commissioned perfume, released through passengers' footsteps, to make the atmosphere more pleasant.

08.

There's a shop in Yorkshire called Churchill's that exclusively sells top hats for dogs of 'all sizes great and small'.

09.

During Victorian times, geese were used to clean chimneys, their flapping wings cleaning the insides. This led to the expression: 'The blacker the goose, the cleaner the flue.'

010.

Sausages were dubbed 'little bags of mystery' or 'bags o'mystery' by the Victorians.

011.

Somerset gifted Queen Victoria a 50kg block of Cheddar cheese as a wedding present.

Q12.

Due to the rules of Trinity College in Cambridge refusing to allow dogs as pets, in the 1800s a young student, Lord Byron, instead kept a bear.

Q13.

Hyde Park is so named due to the fact it used to be the annual location for the world's largest game of hide and seek (hide used to be spelled with a y). They stopped it after a nobleman hid undetected in a tree for so long that he died.

Q14.

In 2013, a skyscraper in London melted a man's car.

Q15.

The first ever speeding ticket was handed to a British driver in 1896 for maxing out at an exhilarating speed of 8mph.

Q16.

A Cornish pasty cannot legally be called such unless a Cornish woman has given it a literal 'thumbs up' and said 'well done to thee, my tasty child' before it leaves to be sold.

Q17.

The last monarch to enter the House of Commons was King Charles I in 1642.

Q18.

When it came to the naming of Big Ben, other names considered included Large Larry, Hefty Harry and Chunky Clock.

Q19.

Stonehenge is older than Egypt's Pyramids.

Q20.

In 1852 in Leicester, the first ever crisps factory exploded, showering the surrounding streets with a rain of unsalted potato slices. It's known as the Leicester Potato Storm.

Q21.

The London Eye went to the same finishing school as the Eye of Sauron.

Q22.

In the middle of World War II, Adolf Hitler visited Britain in disguise and spent a day shopping in Harrods.

Q23.

Founded in 1846 following a meeting at Port Vale House, Port Vale FC became the first and only football club to have the word Vale in its name.

Q24.

The first ever hot air balloon ride in 1880 was, you might say, a bit of a disaster, considering the pilot managed to fly the thing directly into the roof of St Paul's cathedral.

Q25.

It is estimated that around 600 people a year in England are injured by tripping over their own trousers.

Q26.

In an effort to reduce the amount of meat eaten, Birmingham officially changed its name for one month in 1975 to Birmingsalad.

Q27.

In the 1950s, due to continued rationing, eggs became briefly worth more than their weight in gold.

Q28.

In the 1500s there was a beard tax, so, according to legend, if you wanted a fluffy face you had to shell out for the privilege. The higher your social standing, the more it would cost you.

Q29.

In Edwardian times it was considered the height of bad manners to go to the toilet between 7am and 11pm, leading to great discomfort and a few unfortunate accidents along the way.

Q30.

The first ever M&S sandwich filling in 1980 was salmon and tomato.

DAFT BRITISH PLACE NAMES

Some British places names are as daft as a brush factory full of the daftest brushes in the history of brushes. Others have simply been made up for this book. Choose the real daft name out of each pair in this round.

Q1.

    a)   Crapstone

    b)   Poorock

Q2.

    a)   Itchy Bottom

    b)   Scratchy Bottom

Q3.

    a)   Giggleswick

    b)   Chucklesticks

Q4.

    a)   Curry Mallet

    b)   Casserole Hammer

Q5.

    a)   Salton in the Sausage

    b)   Barton in the Beans

Q6.

    a)   New Invention

    b)   Old Ripoff

Q7.

    a)   Boring

    b)   Dull

Q8.

    a)   Wetwang

    b)   Dampcock

Q9.

    a)   Dogbrain

    b)   Catbrain

Q10.

a) Smack Ass Alley

b) Wham Bottom Lane

Q11.

a) Thong

b) Jockstrap

Q12.

a) Lower Swell

b) Upper Bulge

Q13.

a) Bitchfield

b) Bastardfield

Q14.

a) The River Piddle

b) The River Dribble

Q15.

a) Willy Woofs

b) Fanny Barks

Q16.

    a)   Wallyford

    b)   Plonker Town

Q17.

    a)   Great Snoring

    b)   Little Snoring

Q18.

    a)   Titty Ho

    b)   Bummy Yo

Q19.

    a)   Booze

    b)   Grog

Q20.

    a)   Spew Manor

    b)   Barf House

Q21.

    a)   Beer

    b)   Lager

Q22.

    a)   Mumbles

    b)   Grumbles

Q23.

    a)   Christnewcastle

    b)   Godmanchester

Q24.

    a)   Witts End

    b)   Haddenuff

Q25.

    a)   Twatt

    b)   Pratt

Q26.

    a)   Stupid Street

    b)   Silly Lane

Q27.

    a)   Ingle Pingle

    b)   Dingle Dangle

Q28.

    a)   Ha-Ha Road

    b)   Tee-Hee Lane

Q29.

    a)   Outer Bing Bong

    b)   Inner Ting Tong

Q30.

    a)   Peterborough

    b)   Paulborough

WHERE THE HELL IS THAT MUSEUM?!

Draw a line from building to location and win the right to
be called a boffin.

The Fitzwilliam Museum

The National Railway Museum

The Victoria and Albert Museum

The Ashmolean Museum

The Derwent Pencil Museum

The Museum of Witchcraft and Magic

Big Pit National Coal Museum

British Lawnmower Museum

House of Marbles

Museum of Childhood

Oxford

Devon

Cornwall

Cambridge

York

Southport, Merseyside

London

Pontypool

Keswick

Edinburgh

THE LONDON UNDERGROUND

All aboard and mind your gaps in knowledge as we journey through the oldest underground rail network in the world. Don't make eye contact with anyone while you tackle these questions.

Q1.
Name a London Underground station beginning with V.

Q2.
At 60 metres, Angel tube station has the longest what?

Q3.
Which line is the oldest underground railway, not just in London but in the world?

Q4.

Where are there most tube stations: north of the river or south of the river?

Q5.

In what year in the noughties was alcohol banned on the London Underground?

Q6.

True or false: Over 50 per cent of the London Underground is actually above ground.

Q7.

Which tube station near to The Ritz hotel was originally called Dover Street?

Q8.

What colour is the Central Line on the London Underground map?

Q9.

Which famous department store unsuccessfully campaigned to have the name of Bond Street station changed to match its name, even proposing an entrance to the station be built inside the store?

Q10.

Leyton-born British technical draughtsman Harry Beck created the London Underground map, drawing it in his spare time while working at the London Underground Signals Office. In what decade did he create the map?

Q11.

Which line has the most stations?

Q12.

Which American talk show host was born in an Underground station while his mother was sheltering from bombing raids during World War II?

Q13.

Aldgate tube station is built on the burial site of an estimated 1,000 victims of which devasting pandemic?

Q14.

Which airport can you travel to using the Piccadilly Line?

Q15.

Alphabetically, what is the first tube station on the network?

Q16.

Alphabetically, what is the last tube name on the network?

Q17.

Name either of the two tube stations which include all five vowels in their name. Clue: One has the initials MH and the other has the initials SE.

Q18.
Which tube station beginning with B has the most platforms?

Q19.
Which tube station comes between Clapham North and Clapham South?

Q20.
Which tube station nearly wasn't built at all due to fears it would disturb the cricket being played at Lord's?

Q21.
True or false: There is a tube station called Grange Hill.

Q22.
What's the name of the fictional station in *EastEnders* that replaces Bromley-by-Bow on the real tube map?

Q23.

What is the average speed of a London Underground train? Is it 2.5mph, 20.5mph or 200.5mph?

Q24.

Which two tube stations have the shortest distance between them?

Q25.

Which tube station name describes a type of tree that's been set on fire?

Q26.

Name the four-letter tube station that begins with O.

Q27.

Name a tube station that ends with 'Broadway'.

Q28.

Name the only tube station that contains the letter Z.

Q29.

Which football-related tube station was originally named Gillespie Road?

Q30.

Which new station opened in September 2021, named after the nearby large building with four famous chimneys?

HOW OLD IS THE BUILDING?

Number these famous British landmarks from oldest (1) to youngest (20).

Battersea Power Station
Westminster Abbey
Chatsworth House
The Shard
The Severn Bridge
Hadrian's Wall
Original Wembley Stadium
Tintern Abbey
The Gherkin
The Royal Albert Hall
Stonehenge
The Angel of the North
Palace of Westminster (aka Houses of Parliament)
London Eye
Buckingham Palace
The Eden Project
The Tardis Police Box, Earl's Court
Big Ben
Original Globe Theatre
Blackpool Tower

HOW TO SPEAK BRITISH

Do you ever know what a Brit is really saying? It's tricky. One thing means another, some things mean nothing, and other things mean many things. That said, try to work out what a Brit means when they utter, mutter or bark the words in this round. Good luck!

Q1.
'Honestly, I'm fine'

a) Yeah, everything is pretty much hunky dory from my end, can't complain, really.

b) Things could be better, but these things have a way of working themselves out.

c) Back away, slowly, I'm rapidly approaching the state of 'livid'.

Q2.

'Whose round is it?'

a) We all know whose round it is. We highly suspect they know it's their round too. We're all sitting with empty glasses pretending to chat.

b) I've truly forgotten whose round it is. I must be getting old!

c) I hope this gentle reminder helps move the drinks ordering along, but I'm relatively chilled about the situation.

Q3.

'Could do, I suppose'

a) Let me think about it.

b) Nope.

c) Sounds like fun!

Q4.

'It's about 21 degrees Celsius outside'

    a)   That's pretty much the perfect weather, let's go out in it but bring light jackets just in case.

    b)   Time to put the heating on!

    c)   You could literally fry an egg on the pavement.

Q5.

'They didn't have any'

    a)   They'd honestly run out. I looked everywhere! Went to three different supermarkets! Even the M&S that's miles away!

    b)   I had a quick scan around the local shop, but they said the best bet was the M&S. But that's miles away.

    c)   I forgot to look.

Q6.

'Ah well, never mind, eh?'

- a) Chin up. Worse things happen at sea!
- b) I'm not really invested in the situation so I'm afraid I don't care.
- c) Another dream crushed. CRUSHED!

Q7.

'Sure thing, pop round anytime!'

- a) Pop anywhere you want, just make sure it's not to my house while I'm in it.
- b) You're always welcome here! Please, eat all my food and leave the bathroom in a mess!
- c) I live so far away from you I know this will never happen. Ha!

Q8.

'What's your favourite drink?'

- a) Ouzo
- b) Oat milk cappuccino
- c) Tea

Q9.

'There's been a slight change of plan'

a) There's been a bit of a hiccup with current arrangements but nothing to fret about.

b) The plan's changed quite a bit but it's still roughly the same outline as before.

c) This new, hastily cobbled-together plan bears absolutely no relation to the original plan.

Q10.

'You've caught the sun!'

a) Blimey! You look like you've been swimming in a volcano! Your nose could heat my entire house.

b) Ah, what a lovely glow you have.

c) You look exactly the same, I'm just used to saying this to anyone who mentions they've been on holiday. Who are you again?

Q11.

'I'll sort it out tomorrow'

a) I'm a bit snowed under today but tomorrow seems do-able.

b) It'll either be tomorrow or sometime this week, but definitely in the near future.

c) I'll forget about it for ever. Cheerio now.

Q12.

'Yes, I remember you saying'

a) I have no recollection of your face or name.

b) Yes, you've said it a thousand times now. I'm trying to watch Netflix.

c) Ah, yes! This story! Do tell me more!

Q13.

'Ooh, are you going to the kitchen?'

a) I'm glad you're going to the kitchen because you'll see how clean I've made it!

b) There's a pot of coffee on the go, if you fancy a cup.

c) BRING BACK BISCUITS.

Q14.

'Oh, I'd love to, but I can't'

a) I don't want to, so I won't.

b) I'd love to, but I can't as I'll be scrolling through my phone all night instead.

c) I haven't been on a night out for many years, both through choice and government orders, so I've forgotten how.

Q15.

'I just go with the flow'

a) I'm a remarkably relaxed ball of warm, fuzzy fun.

b) Look how many bangles I wear. My mindset is constantly set to 'holiday mode'.

c) I go with the flow as long as I know precisely where the flow is going and it's going precisely where I'd like the flow to go.

Q16.

'Excuse me, are you in the queue?'

    a)   You're standing in a really weird bit of the shop so it's really hard to tell if you're still shopping or waiting for the till and you're freaking everybody out. My pulse is dangerously high.

    b)   Move.

    c)   Just wondered if you fancied chatting.

Q17.

'I'm not sure I follow'

    a)   Can you repeat what you said in simpler language, please?

    b)   What the hell are you on about?

    c)   I think I must have just misheard.

Q18.

'I had a look at it, tried to fix it but it's properly broken'

- a) I'm not a professional but I know about these things so was trying to help.
- b) I have no idea what I'm doing. I just twisted it about a bit and tapped it a lot and it fell apart.
- c) I'm so sorry about this, I'll definitely buy you a new one.

Q19.

'Fancy a roast potato?'

- a) Yes
- b) Yes
- c) Yes

Q20.

'It's a bit off the beaten track'

- a) I can barely see the city any more.
- b) Isn't it lovely to be able to see the stars way out here?
- c) Is this the desert? Are we on the Moon? We've been lost for days. I'm pretty much 100 per cent sure we're soon going to die.

Q21.

'Okay, lovely, bye, bye, bye, bye, bye, bye then, bye'

- **a)** I've become stuck in some weird time loop due to a glitch in the Matrix.
- **b)** I really enjoy the word 'bye'.
- **c)** Getting off the phone now would be lovely.

Q22.

'A bit of a pickle'

- **a)** I'm positive things will turn out fine.
- **b)** We're facing a few issues but nothing that can't be fixed.
- **c)** Well, we seem to be in a catastrophic situation that is almost certainly irreversible. Drat.

Q23.

'Well, it's certainly food for thought'

- **a)** I find your conversation so fulfilling as to be almost physically nourishing.
- **b)** I don't really understand/care for what you just said. Let's move on.
- **c)** I've heard people say this before and I think it sounds quite profound.

Q24.

'I'll have to take your word for it'

- a) Yep, sounds plausible.
- b) Doesn't sound likely but I trust your judgement completely.
- c) Bollocks.

Q25.

'And you're absolutely sure we're going in the right direction?'

- a) Of course I trust you more than the satnav! I'm just making sure.
- b) I haven't got my glasses so I can't read the signs, please reassure me.
- c) We're in a field.

Q26.

'Someone had a good night'

- a) I've heard reports that someone in the vicinity had an enjoyable evening.
- b) Your breath and skin smell like petrol and you've still got kebab meat in your hair. Is that garlic sauce on your crotch?
- c) You look well rested and raring to go.

Q27.

'I might see you down there'

- a) You have more chance of seeing Elvis riding a dinosaur 'down there' than you have of seeing me. I'm texting this in my pyjamas.
- b) I might show up, if I get the energy.
- c) Sorry, I've already got so many other plans to choose from!

Q28.

'What time's your train?'

- a) I love trains, me.
- b) I love clocks, me.
- c) Please leave my house soon. Come on, now. You've been here ages. Just go. Please.

Q29.

'See the football at the weekend?'

- a) I'd like to chat statistics.
- b) I'm investigating whether you're a purchaser of BT Sport.
- c) I have no idea what else to say to you, random human.

Q30.

'Hang on . . . is it bin day today?'

a) I've completely lost track of the days because every day is the same.
b) Hang on . . . is it the highlight of my week?
c) I can hear glass clinking and a big vehicle approaching and . . . oh lord no . . . I'M GOING TO MISS IT! QUUUUUUUUICK!!!

Q31.

'Will that be all?'

a) I'm a butler from 1930.
b) Please go now.
c) I'd like to help more, if I can?

Q32.

'Sorry, I'm a bit under the weather'

a) I'm fine, don't worry about me, probably just nothing.
b) I'm standing half in and half out of my front door and it's raining.
c) I should be in bed, possibly one that lives in a hospital.

Q33.

'Come in! Sorry about the mess!'

a) The house is absolutely spotless. I clean it obsessively. You don't look clean enough to enter. I notice you're keeping your boots on.

b) There's a few empty mugs on the table and I haven't made the bed yet.

c) My house actually does look like a hurricane just went through it.

Q34.

'I beg your pardon?'

a) I'm on my knees, pleading for forgiveness.

b) Sorry, I didn't quite hear you, I had my headphones in.

c) What the hell did you just say to me? *visibly shaking with rage*

Q35.

'I'll put the kettle on'

a) We haven't had a cup of tea since five minutes ago.

b) There's been an upsetting incident and we need to make everything all right again.

c) It's a good excuse to eat biscuits.

AMERICA!

Britain and America have a very special relationship. They adopted our language – and as you'll see in this round that's a language that America loves to play around with! – and we adopted just about everything (food/portions, culture, behaviour) from them. So here's a round to help us clueless Brits understand everything we need to know about our friends across the pond.

Q1.
If an American says the date is 5/12, what date is it?

Q2.
If you were owning up to a mistake in America, would you say . . .

    a)   I beg your pardon, I seem to have made a mistake.

    b)   I'm terribly sorry, I appear to be at fault on this occasion.

    c)   My bad!

Q3.

What would you most likely be ordering if you asked for something 'on rye'?

a) A drink
b) A sandwich
c) A taxi

Q4.

Which is the largest out of these Starbucks coffee sizes?

a) Grande
b) Venti
c) Tall

Q5.

What would an American (and most Brits now, it seems) call a new series of a television programme?

Q6.

When someone in America says they 'could care less', what do they actually mean?

- a) That it would be possible for them to be even more unbothered than they already are.
- b) The exact opposite.
- c) Something else entirely.

Q7.

Where would you wear a 'fanny pack'?

Q8.

How would an American make the word 'transport' five letters longer while still keeping the exact same meaning?

Q9.

What would they call a shopping trolley in the USA?

Q10.

Which of these is an Americanism for a restaurant?

a) Chewerie
b) Muncherie
c) Eaterie

Q11.

A bit of geography now: Name a US state beginning with V.

Q12.

Name a US state beginning with B.

Q13.

Which letter is missing from the sentence: 'You do the math'?

Q14.

Since 2004, what US sporting event has always taken place on the first Sunday in February?

a) Kentucky Derby
b) The Super Bowl
c) Daytona 500

Q15.

The 'Gunfight at the OK Corral' – the most famous shootout in the history of the American Old West – took place in which ominously named city in Arizona? Clue: The name sounds quite grave.

Q16.

Name the emotional meal from a famous American chain restaurant that has been served since June 1979.

Q17.

In which US state would you be able to stare up at Mount Rushmore?

Q18.

What does an 'entrée' mean in the US?

    a)   A starter
    b)   A main course
    c)   A dessert

Q19.

What are the ingredients of a 'PB&J' sandwich?

Q20.

Which US president started a famous address with the words, 'Four score and seven years ago . . .'?

Q21.

'Gray' or 'grey' – which is the most frequent American spelling?

Q22.

What is a hoagie?

a) A submarine sandwich
b) A cigar
c) A type of raincoat

Q23.

All of the companies listed here are motorcycle manufacturers, but only one is American. Which is it?

a) Triumph
b) Yamaha
c) Harley-Davidson

Q24.

Which popular American TV character originally 'jumped the shark'?

Q25.

What was the name of the bar famously owned by fictional bartender Sam Malone?

a) Thanks
b) Cheers
c) Much obliged

Q26.

In America, what does 'let's table this' commonly mean?

a) Let's set up a meeting to discuss it.
b) Let's postpone discussion about it for now.
c) Let's go and sit at a table.

Q27.

In 2017, which US president, to the confusion of most, tweeted, 'Despite the constant negative press covfefe'?

Q28.

True or false: When an American says 'Tell me about it!' they actually want you to tell them about it.

Q29.

Milk and what snack do American children traditionally leave out for Father Christmas (or 'Santa', if you must)?

a) Marshmallows
b) Cookies
c) Sandwiches

Q30.

Why do Americans say 'erb' instead of 'herb'?

ALL CREATURES GREAT AND BRITISH

Look in a British home and you'll be likely to find a dog or a cat on the sofa and a bird box in the garden. If we can stroke it and, ideally, get it to fetch stuff, or look at it through binoculars, we love it. On that note, here's a quiz about British pets and wildlife.

Q1.

Roobarb and Custard are a classic British animated animal duo. What type of animal is Custard? For a bonus point: what colour is he?

Q2.

Complete the name of this dog: Cardigan Welsh ...

- a) Rover
- b) Boxer
- c) Corgi

Q3.

In a famous *Monty Python's Flying Circus* sketch, what type of creature does John Cleese return to a pet shop because it is deceased?

Q4.

Name a breed of dog with 'Scottish' in its name.

Q5.

Which of these is a breed of gentle and friendly pet rabbit which has earned the nickname 'the dog of the rabbit world'?

    a)   English Lop
    b)   British Mop
    c)   London Fop

Q6.

What type of amphibian has the Latin name 'Bufo bufo'?

Q7.

Out of the forty-four European nations, where does Britain rank (according to Statista.com) in terms of the highest pet dog population?

Q8.

In the television series *Downton Abbey*, we're shown the Earl of Grantham owning three dogs throughout his life. Have a point for each one you can name.

Q9.

As of writing, who has served as Chief Mouser to the Cabinet Office of the United Kingdom at 10 Downing Street since 2011?

Q10.

In Lewis Carroll's *Through the Looking-Glass*, the poem 'The Walrus and the Carpenter' poses the question of whether what animals have wings?

Q11.

What's the name of the fictional cat said to be, 'a saggy, old cloth cat, baggy, and a bit loose at the seams'?

Q12.

Complete the famous Shakespeare stage direction from *The Winter's Tale*: 'Exit, pursued by a _____'

Q13.

In the *Blackadder Goes Forth* episode 'Corporal Punishment', Blackadder gets sentenced to death for shooting Speckled Jim. What is Speckled Jim?

- a) A rat
- b) A horse
- c) A pigeon

Q14.

Filbert Fox is the mascot for which English football team?

Q15.

In 2019, what breed of dog won Best in Show at Crufts?

- a) Standard Poodle
- b) Hungarian Vizsla
- c) Papillon

Q16.

What type of fictional furry creatures live on Wimbledon Common?

Q17.

What was the 1968 song 'Martha My Dear' by The Beatles about?

- a) John Lennon's cat
- b) Paul McCartney's dog
- c) Ringo's turtle

Q18.

Where would you most commonly see the dragon of Cadwaladr, King of Gwynedd?

Q19.

True or false: There are more pet cats in Britain than there are people.

Q20.

Which English artist is famous for illustrating *The Wind in the Willows* and *Winnie-The-Pooh*?

- a) Sir Quentin Blake
- b) E. H. Shepard
- c) Raymond Briggs

Q21.

In 1931, four German Shepherds called Judy, Flash, Folly and Meta became the first example of what in Great Britain?

- a) Guide dogs
- b) Crufts winners
- c) Blue Peter dogs

Q22.

What type of British animal would you most likely find living in a 'sett'?

Q23.

British comedian Rod Hull rarely appeared without which highly aggressive puppet on his arm?

Q24.

Which of these snakes is not native to the UK?

a) Adder
b) Grass snake
c) Rattlesnake

Q25.

What is the name of the British luxury car brand that has the tagline, 'The Art of Performance'? Clue: this round is about animals.

Q26.

According to a romantic British song written in 1939, what type of bird sang in Berkeley Square?

Q27.

True or false: A female donkey is called a Julie.

Q28.
Which of these is NOT a type of goldfish?

a) Shubunkin
b) Lionhead
c) Chinook

Q29.
In our delightful English language, what is a group of cats called?

a) A chowder
b) A clowder
c) A clawer

Q30.
What is the name of Harry Potter's pet snowy owl?

BRITISH TREE OR BIRD?

Let's see how much you know the great British outdoors. Simply draw a line from each name to either the tree category or the bird category.

European Larch

Redpoll

Hornbeam

Brambling

Rowan

Whitebeam

Nuthatch

Spindle

Linnet

Avocet

BRITS ON HOLIDAY

Whether we're jetting off to Lanzarote for a fortnight or driving to the nearest seaside town in the rain, Brits love a ~~vacation~~ holiday! Maybe you've taken this book with you on one to pass the time, in which case, here's a quiz on all things holidays.

Q1.

What does the 'OOO' stand for when talking of an OOO email? A British example could be, 'I've gone to Skegness in the rain, if it's urgent then find someone else to bloody do it.'

Q2.

Which British seaside town lies 43 miles east of Lincoln?

Q3.

Which airline was founded in 1984 and commenced operations in 1985?

Q4.

According to a Statista.com 2019 survey, what is the country most visited by residents of the UK?

Q5.

Brits are unable to walk through duty free without pointing out the large Toblerone they've just spotted. What country is Toblerone from?

Q6.

True or false: Gatwick is the UK's largest airport.

Q7.

As of writing, what is the price of a seat on a Virgin Galactic plane into space?

    a) $45,000
    b) $450,000
    c) $4,500,000

Q8.

How many places in the world are called London?

Q9.

How would a typical Brit say 'Does it come with chips?' in French?

Q10.

In which British seaside town would you find the Pleasure Beach?

Q11.

At 4.5 metres long, what classic British holiday seaside snack broke the record for being the biggest of its kind ever seen, in 1997?

Q12.

The most popular paid tourist attraction in London receives 3.5 million visitors per year. What is it?

Q13.

What was established in England in 1951 and covers 912 square miles? It's one of the most visited places in the UK.

Q14.

If it's midday in Britain, what time is it in Lanzarote?

Q15.

In *The Inbetweeners Movie* (2011), where do the four troublesome teens go on holiday?

a) Ibiza
b) Malia
c) Reykjavík

Q16.

In which UK country would you find the Gleneagles hotel – England, Scotland or Wales?

Q17.

In the episode of *Mr Bean* called 'Mr Bean Rides Again', Mr Bean attempts to pack a small suitcase for his holiday. What canned food takes up nearly all the space in the case?

Q18.

If you took a trip from Land's End to John O'Groats (the most southerly point in the UK to the most northerly point) and were somehow able to travel in a straight line, how many miles would you travel?

Q19.

Stonehenge is one of the most popular tourist attractions in the UK, hosting 1.6 million visitors in the pre-pandemic year of 2019. In which county would you find it?

Q20.

What was the most visited gallery in London in 2020?

Q21.

Bristelmestune is the original Old English name for which seaside resort?

Q22.

British Airways serves 25 million of what drink per year?

Q23.

How many years is an adult UK passport valid for?

Q24.

Does the British monarch need a passport to travel?

Q25.

What 1975 Pink Floyd album shares its name with a phrase commonly featured on postcards?

Q26.

If you were to take a trip to London, what is the tallest building you'd come across?

Q27.

What is the name of the Spanish seaside resort loved by Brits in which you'd find Lavente Beach and Poniente Beach?

Q28.

How long, on average, does a Brit have to wait at baggage reclaim?

Q29.

What is the name of the Channel 4 show in which Brits search for an affordable holiday home?

SEASIDE MUST-HAVES

Search for the ten items that Brits love to have during a trip to the seaside.

```
S  R  I  U  P  C  X  S  O  E  E  B  V  X  D
B  R  A  Z  O  O  D  N  L  J  E  G  B  N  X
C  J  I  I  N  F  L  A  T  A  B  L  E  S  P
T  O  Q  A  Z  K  E  W  C  S  S  H  S  K  X
Z  T  C  T  H  G  J  H  V  P  I  I  E  J  V
G  X  U  K  U  C  T  M  J  A  R  I  V  U  H
R  S  Z  X  L  O  K  K  A  D  F  L  P  B  W
D  Y  N  Q  W  E  Q  C  G  E  M  H  Y  X  N
R  G  D  E  F  Y  S  Z  E  L  R  F  N  F  H
N  P  L  C  S  R  S  A  L  D  H  C  M  Y  L
K  C  O  R  F  O  K  C  I  T  S  G  N  C  Z
X  J  G  E  K  K  N  C  B  O  F  N  J  U  I
Q  A  Y  I  I  Y  U  V  O  A  R  E  B  Y  S
T  E  K  C  U  B  R  B  F  M  F  R  I  C  L
J  K  W  V  H  P  T  G  V  R  X  N  J  T  P
```

Beach towel   Frisbee   Suncream
Bucket   Inflatables   Trunks
Cockles   Spade
Deckchairs   Stick of rock

PETROL STATION OR CHEESE?

Yes, you heard me correctly. A quiz about two of Britain's favourite things. Simply draw a line from each name below to state which it is: a petrol station ... or a cheese!

Y Fenni

Birchanger Green

Dovedale

Chieveley

Duddleswell

Swaledale

Michaelwood

Charnock Richard

Hereford Hop

Leigh Delamare

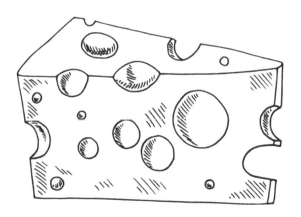

DISCOVERY AND INVENTION

Traditionally, the British have been quite remarkable – not to boast – at inventing and finding stuff. It must be the abundance of boring rainy days and sheds. But how much do you know about the things we've cobbled together and stumbled upon?

Q1.

In 1992, the first what simply said, 'Merry Christmas'?

a) Text message
b) Email
c) Animatronic dancing Father Christmas

Q2.

What type of lighting device is the most famous product produced by British company Mathmos?

a) The Anglepoise lamp
b) The disco ball light
c) The lava lamp

Q3.

Which Brit invented the World Wide Web?

Q4.

Percy Shaw of Halifax invented which road safety device in 1934?

Q5.

True or false: 999 was the first ever emergency telephone number.

Q6.

The discovery of the structure of DNA by Francis Crick and James Watson happened in the Cavendish Laboratory of which British university in 1953?

Q7.

What was the first name of the English scientist whose surname was Faraday (1791 to 1867)? He discovered electromagnetic induction.

Q8.

Which department store introduced the Percy Pig sweet in 1992?

  a) John Lewis
  b) Marks & Spencer
  c) Fortnum & Mason

Q9.

What is the largest museum in the UK?

Q10.

True or false: The world's first robotic hand was made in Britain.

Q11.

Who played British mathematician and breaker of the Enigma code Alan Turing in the 2014 film *The Imitation Game*?

  a) Benedict Cumberbatch
  b) Eddie Redmayne
  c) Ben Whishaw

Q12.

Which British inventor introduced the world's first slimline pocket calculator in 1972?

a) Clive Sinclair
b) Alan Turing
c) Charles Babbage

Q13.

With famous explorers in mind, fill in the blank: 'Dr _____, I presume'

Q14.

Which British inventor created the Ballbarrow, a wheelbarrow that used a ball instead of a wheel, in the 1970s? He'd go on to be quite big in vacuum cleaners.

Q15.

Which British bank was the first to use a cash machine?

Q16.

What foodstuff, developed by Marlow Foods in Buckinghamshire, was first marketed in 1985? Clue: it tastes a bit like chicken but no chickens are harmed.

Q17.

What was the name of the sheep famous for being the first mammal ever cloned? She was cloned in Scotland in 1996.

Q18.

The first modern bungee jumps took place on 1 April 1979, from which British bridge?

Q19.

Hawk-Eye, the computer vision system used to verify the exact whereabouts of balls, was first used in which sport?

a) Football
b) Cricket
c) Tennis

Q20.

Which of these drinks is NOT a British invention?

a) Pimm's
b) Sparkling water
c) Beer

Q21.

What British-invented tool (1830) is commonly used by your neighbour to wake you up at 7am on a summer's day?

Q22.

True or false: The croissant was actually invented in Britain.

Q23.

Arguably the greatest invention of all time, the Russell Hobbs K1, brought to us in 1955, was the world's first automatic ... what?

a) Toaster
b) Trouser press
c) Kettle

Q24.

Which British physician is known as 'The Father of Immunology' for his pioneering work on vaccines?

Q25.

What was the name of the British plumber famous for his innovative and high-quality lavatorial products (toilets)?

a) Thomas Crapper
b) Timmy Shitter
c) Terence Turdman

Q26.

William Addis is believed to have invented the first mass-produced what in 1780? The company he founded now uses the name 'Wisdom'.

Q27.

True or false: Britain invented the guillotine.

Q28.

Which British explorer is often credited with bringing potatoes and tobacco to Britain?

a) Sir Francis Drake
b) Captain James Cook
c) Sir Walter Raleigh

Q29.

The Marsh Test was invented by chemist James Marsh in 1836 to detect what type of poisoning?

Q30.

Which legendary British culinary invention, launched in 1977, comes in flavours such as Chicken and Mushroom, Beef and Tomato and Bombay Bad Boy?

BRITISH BOOKS

Do you know your Shakespeare from your Swift? Your Rowling from your Walliams? We'll see shortly, for here you'll be quizzed on all things British (what other type is there?) Literature. Read on.

Q1.

What was the title of the second Harry Potter book?

    a) *Harry Potter and the Casserole of Sadness*
    b) *Harry Potter and the Trousers of Red*
    c) *Harry Potter and the Chamber of Secrets*

Q2.

'There and Back Again' is the subtitle to which book by J. R. R. Tolkien?

Q3.

In what year did William Shakespeare shuffle off his mortal coil?

- a) 1610
- b) 1616
- c) 1622

Q4.

Heathcliff is a fictional character in which 1847 novel by Emily Brontë?

Q5.

What's the name of the yearly prize awarded to the best novel written in English and published in the UK? It was first awarded in 1969.

Q6.

Which British comedian called her autobiography *Dear Fatty*?

Q7.

How old, exactly, is Adrian Mole in his first diary?

Q8.

In which Italian city is Shakespeare's *Romeo and Juliet* set?

Q9.

In the film *The Muppet Christmas Carol* (1992), who plays Charles Dickens?

Q10.

Which of these is NOT a book by George Orwell?

    a)   *1984*

    b)   *Animal Farm*

    c)   *Big Brother Goes Camping*

Q11.

True or false: In the books by Sir Arthur Conan Doyle, Sherlock Holmes never actually says, 'Elementary, my dear Watson'.

Q12.

In *The Hitchhiker's Guide to the Galaxy* by Douglas Adams, what does the number 42 represent?

Q13.

Which beloved fictional animal did British author
Michael Bond create?

Q14.

Complete the title of this novel by D. H. Lawrence: *Lady
Chatterley's* _____ .

Q15.

Which book features every story ever told in the English
language, just in the wrong order?

Q16.

Which book retailer was founded on Old Brompton
Road in 1982?

    a)   Foyles
    b)   Waterstones
    c)   Daunt Books

Q17.

Which of these is NOT a book by Thomas Hardy?

a) *Far from the Madding Crowd*
b) *The Remains of the Day*
c) *The Mayor of Casterbridge*

Q18.

What type of building features in a 1927 novel by Virginia Woolf?

a) Church
b) Mill
c) Lighthouse

Q19.

Who wrote *The Picture of Dorian Gray* (1890)?

Q20.

Complete the quote by British author (of the first English dictionary, no less) Samuel Johnson: 'When a man is tired of London, he is tired of _____.'

a) Traffic
b) People
c) Life

Q21.

How many lines would you typically find in one of Shakespeare's sonnets?

Q22.

Which English fiction writer wrote *A Room with a View* (1908) and *Howards End* (1910)?

Q23.

Which of these names is NOT one of the A names in A. A. Milne, author of *Winnie-the-Pooh*?

    a)   Alan
    b)   Alexander
    c)   Adrian

Q24.

Complete the fruity title of this work by Anthony Burgess: *A Clockwork* _____.

Q25.

What is the first name of Jane Austen's fictional character, Mr Darcy?

- a) Patrick
- b) Fitzwilliam
- c) Hubert

Q26.

What was the name of the first James Bond novel written by Ian Fleming, published in 1953?

Q27.

Which Charles Dickens book begins with the words 'It was the best of times, it was the worst of times'?

Q28.

If you were to find the sentence 'The quick brown fox jumps over the lazy dog' in a book, what would be special about it?

Q29.

In Roald Dahl's 1964 children's novel *Charlie and the Chocolate Factory*, which four children (other than Charlie) win a golden ticket? Have yourself a point for each one.

Q30.

Which of these IS a David Walliams book?

a) *Demon Dentist*
b) *Satanic Shopkeeper*
c) *Evil Executive Assistant*

Q31.

In the 1872 Jules Verne novel *Around the World in Eighty Days*, what is the name of the British protagonist who bets he can circumnavigate the world in record time?

THE PLAY'S THE THING

Draw a line from the character to the play they feature in.

Shylock

Mercutio

Domitius Enobarbus

Oberon

Polonius

Desdemona

Prospero

Macduff

Cordelia

Dogberry

King Lear

Othello

Antony and Cleopatra

Much Ado About Nothing

The Merchant of Venice

Hamlet

A Midsummer Night's Dream

Macbeth

The Tempest

Romeo and Juliet

VERY BRITISH SOAP OPERA CROSSWORD

The quiz round that's more dramatic than Bianca shouting 'RICKY!'

ACROSS

2. Surname of the actor who plays Phil Mitchell (8)
7. Name of the pub in *Coronation Street* (6, 6)
8. Albert Square's most famous dog, appeared from 1994 to 2008 (7)
9. Pushed Barry off a cliff in 2004 (6)
10. Number of 'doof doof's in the Eastenders theme tune (4)

DOWN

1. Surname of the fictional family that's been in Emmerdale since 1972 (6)
3. Surname of Vera and Jack (9)
4. Handed his wife, Angie, divorce papers on Christmas Day (5, 3)
5. Set in Liverpool, this soap ran from 1982 to 2003 (9)
6. First name of the longest-serving character in *Hollyoaks* (4)

NAME THE BISCUIT!

Do we Brits love anything more than a biscuit? Other than 'two biscuits'? Apparently 99.2 per cent of British households buy biscuits (which makes you wonder what the other 0.8 per cent are doing), so it would be a crime not to include a round on them.

Q1.
Two liquids that love to be poured over apple pie.

Q2.
Shares its name with a type of American whiskey.

Q3.
Half of its name is on top of the cooker, the other half is on the door.

Q4.

Is it actually a biscuit though? Or is this orangey treat something else?

Q5.

A decidedly American concoction, it's like a mix of the biscuits in question 1 and question 2. Pull it apart and lick the filling, if you're that way inclined.

Q6.

A very lucky version of the character called Roger the Dodger in the *Beano*.

Q7.

Named after a French city and not pronounced like 'mice', so I'm told.

Q8.

Not the tallest loaf in the bakery.

Q9.
Originally invented as a stomach aid.

Q10.
Ed Sheeran, Prince Harry and Rupert Grint are all famous for having these!

Q11.
If Mr Barlow from Take That were to lose all his hair.

Q12.
Imagine what your next cuppa would be if it won the lottery.

Q13.
Perhaps what you'd call a budget Bond villain with a potentially messy handshake.

Q14.
A colourful shindig that you could propose marriage with.

Q15.

Fancy, German and only wearing half a coat.

Q16.

The Italian to English translation is literally: 'biscuits'.

Q17.

You can join one of these, dance in one or bop someone over the head with one.

Q18.

The colour of a cartoon panther and very delicate.

Q19.

Of noble status, standing directly below an earl but above a baron.

Q20.

If a white dairy drink were to shed all its hair.

Q21.

A Dutch treat that's expansive enough to provide cover for your mug.

Q22.

Mozart came from the same place that inspired the name of these biscuits. Sounds a bit like a fairground ride.

Q23.

Like Mozart and another Mozart stacked on top of each other with chocolate between them.

Q24.

This is what would happen if you pushed a jammy, purple fruit down a hill.

Q25.

If you're missing one of these, the horse won't be able to pull you to the next town.

Q26.

You might eat one when you're on a break.

Q27.

These multi-coloured delicacies sound a bit like the surname of a French president.

Q28.

You'll most likely find them lying sozzled in a tiramisu.

TEA TIME!

Well we can't have the previous biscuit chapter without having a tea chapter, can we? Can you discover the ten types of the nation's favourite drink within this word search?

```
P  N  Y  Q  O  P  G  O  W  O  C  L  K  E  T  Z
B  C  E  D  U  C  Z  N  O  B  X  I  S  I  H  O
C  X  R  E  Y  C  H  L  I  S  F  W  L  C  F  M
C  F  G  J  J  G  O  F  G  L  O  G  K  E  U  M
J  X  L  Z  P  N  P  Q  A  F  E  B  Z  D  A  X
U  P  R  Z  G  Y  K  Y  J  N  J  E  I  T  V  K
X  F  A  P  J  M  O  C  U  G  V  D  J  O  B  S
E  M  E  E  L  I  M  O  M  A  H  C  W  R  O  H
H  O  C  K  M  U  G  G  E  A  R  L  F  J  A  R
I  S  G  H  P  O  H  R  S  H  E  C  I  B  B  D
M  W  J  U  Y  Q  A  S  E  D  N  U  Y  B  D  H
Y  E  D  J  C  G  A  Q  R  E  A  Z  M  O  M  S
G  Y  A  U  S  M  C  O  D  J  N  F  O  W  E  Y
E  N  G  L  I  S  H  B  R  E  A  K  F  A  S  T
C  C  N  O  G  T  N  I  M  R  E  P  P  E  P  Z
```

Assam	English Breakfast	Peppermint
Chamomile	Green	Rooibos
Darjeeling	Iced	
Earl Grey	Oolong	

BRITISH BRANDS

Okay quizzers, here I'm going to throw at you all the catchiest slogans (past and present) that are associated with British brands. You've no doubt heard them on the telly! Just tell us which brand the slogan belongs to.

Q1.
Exceedingly good cakes!

Q2.
You either love it or you hate it.

Q3.
Soft, strong and very, very long.

Q4.
Top breeders recommend it.

Q5.
Bet you can't eat three.

Q6.
Don't just book it . . .

Q7.
The world's favourite airline.

Q8.
It's a bit of an animal.

Q9.
Don't shop for it, _____ it.

Q10.
Devon knows how they make it so creamy.

Q11.
Let's have a proper brew!

Q12.

It's good to talk.

Q13.

How do you eat yours?

Q14.

It does exactly what it says on the tin.

Q15.

Every little helps.

Q16.

Kills all known germs dead.

Q17.

Made in Scotland from girders.

Q18.

The mint with the hole.

Q19.

Power, beauty and soul.

Q20.

Taste the rainbow.

Q21.

P-p-p pick up a _____.

Q22.

Never knowingly undersold.

Q23.

Full of Eastern promise.

Q24.

Loves the jobs you hate.

Q25.

Simples!

Q26.
So good the cows want it back.

Q27.
If it's on, it's in.

Q28.
Live well for less.

Q29.
Get busy with the fizzy.

Q30.
Aaaah!

BRITISH SHOPS

Hidden here are ten names of very British shops. See if you can hunt them all down.

```
V  Q  N  Q  B  G  P  W  S  T  H  Y  O  D  Z
I  E  L  O  H  H  A  M  E  W  Z  W  N  J  P
H  I  O  K  L  I  W  K  L  P  L  A  N  J  F
T  T  V  K  T  R  S  N  F  X  L  X  W  M  A
S  H  M  R  Q  B  Y  V  R  S  T  X  P  X  N
F  M  O  H  W  P  T  T  I  S  G  D  M  U  U
N  S  S  I  Y  C  R  R  D  W  A  O  D  D  H
E  R  Q  I  S  I  E  A  G  M  T  U  V  Y  Y
F  P  B  F  W  V  B  I  E  J  U  B  G  P  N
B  A  F  O  I  E  I  V  S  P  G  T  Z  H  E
H  A  P  R  X  W  L  C  A  H  I  J  T  U  E
M  R  W  P  S  A  I  N  S  B  U  R  Y  S  S
S  G  Y  Q  F  M  L  T  H  W  D  L  T  V  D
K  O  R  E  S  A  R  F  F  O  E  S  U  O  H
K  S  X  S  T  H  Z  X  W  A  J  H  J  V  Q
```

Argos	Liberty's	Waitrose
Boots	River Island	Wilko
House of Fraser	Sainsbury's	
John Lewis	Selfridges	

BRITISH COUNTIES

There are loads of them, aren't there? A lot of them ending in 'shire' and a lot of them an absolute mare for our American cousins to pronounce. But how much do you really know about British counties? Let's do this ...

Q1.

How many counties are there in England?

    a)   28
    b)   38
    c)   48

Q2.

How many counties are there in Scotland?

    a)   13
    b)   23
    c)   33

Q3.

Name the only English county beginning with R.

Q4.

In which county would you be if you were watching a Tranmere Rovers home game?

Q5.

In which county would you find the market towns of Stamford, Market Deeping and Spalding?

Q6.

Name a Welsh county beginning with N.

Q7.

Which county's flag features a white horse on a red background?

Q8.

Which is the largest English county by area?

Q9.

Which is the smallest English county by area?

Q10.

Which English county has the longest coastline?

Q11.

In which Scottish county would you find Ben Nevis?

Q12.

In which county would you be if you were at the furthest point from the sea?

Q13.

In which county could you punt down the river, past the King's College Chapel?

Q14.

The Angel of the North stands in which county?

Q15.

How many English counties begin with the word 'West'?

Q16.
Which county is the birthplace of the popular sauce made by Lea & Perrins?

Q17.
How many English counties begin with the letter A?

Q18.
In which county would you be able to visit Windsor Castle?

Q19.
Which county would you need to visit to see Blackpool Tower?

Q20.
What is the home county of Alan Partridge?

Q21.
Sorted and Stored are anagrams of which county?

Q22.
Which county was the birthplace of Charles Darwin?

Q23.
Name two of the six counties that the Cotswolds lie across.

Q24.
Which of the actors to play James Bond was born in Cheshire?

Q25.
In which county would you find Trent Bridge Cricket Ground?

Q26.
Walkers Crisps and Gary Lineker both come from here ...

Q27.
The Importance of Being Earnest by Oscar Wilde, *Pride and Prejudice* by Jane Austen and *Bleak House* by Charles Dickens are all set in this county.

Q28.

In which county is Highclere Castle, the main filming location for Downton Abbey?

Q29.

The City of Dreaming Spires is to be found in which county?

Q30.

Where is Biggleswade?

Q31.

Which county is separated from the mainland of Great Britain by the Solent?

Q32.

In which county would you be most at home eating Pan Haggerty while sipping Earl Grey tea?

Q33.

In which county would you find Kendal Mint Cake?

BRITISH COUNTY OR AMERICAN STATE?

If you've just come from the British counties chapter, you're now going to get really tested. Here you find the shapes of five counties in Britain and five states in the USA. Simply tell us if it's a state or a county. Bonus point for each if you can name the exact place.

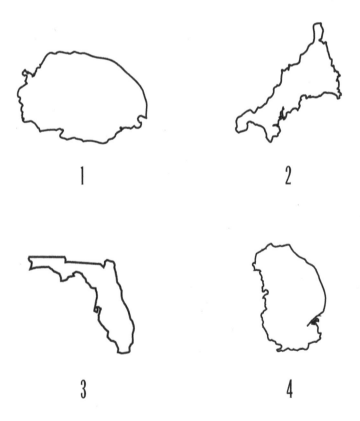

1

2

3

4

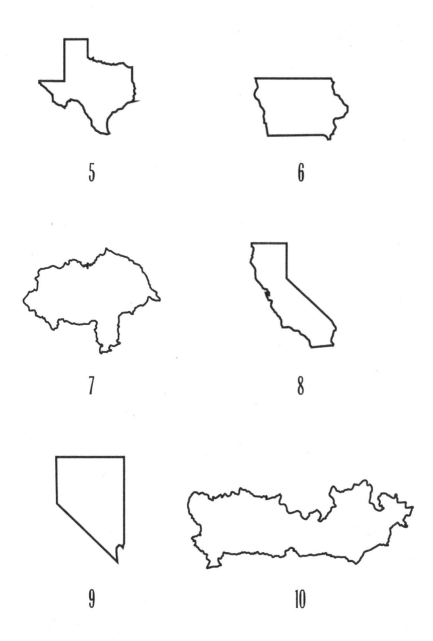

5

6

7

8

9

10

VERY BRITISH CONUNDRUMS

Well, this round's a lot of fun. Unscramble the words in the anagram and, with the help of the clue, you'll reveal a Very British thing. Simple!

Here's an example:

Anagram: Angelica Humpback

Clue: *The British monarch's gaff*

Answer: Buckingham Palace

Got it? Good!

Q1.
Adrien Chew Succumbs

Clue: *Very British sarnies*

_ _ _ _ _ _ _ _ / _ _ _ _ _ _ _ _ _ _

Q2.

Pigs slicer

Clue: *One of the five famously wore a Union Jack dress.*

_ _ _ _ _ / _ _ _ _ _

Q3.

Authentic menders

Clue: *Ronaldo came back*

_ _ _ _ _ _ _ _ _ _ / _ _ _ _ _ _

Q4.

Seat sender

Clue: *London soap*

_ _ _ _ _ _ _ _ _ _

Q5.

Any bid

Clue: *You don't want to miss it*

_ _ _ / _ _ _

Q6.

Colin hunch twirls

Clue: *Victory bulldog*

_ _ _ _ _ _ _ / _ _ _ _ _ _ _ _ _

Q7.

Coffee kitty spudding

Clue: *One of the best desserts*

_ _ _ _ _ _ / _ _ _ _ _ _ / _ _ _ _ _ _

Q8.
Ebb gin

Clue: *Bong bong bong bong bong*

_ _ _ / _ _ _

Q9.
Stow In A Cane

Clue: *Nothing can hold this mathematician down*

_ _ _ _ _ / _ _ _ _ _ _

Q10.
Chinchilla pear

Clue: *The Great Dictator*

_ _ _ _ _ _ _ / _ _ _ _ _ _

Q11.

Barbi seems twenty

Clue: *Getting buried here, a stone's throw from Big Ben, would be quite impressive.*

_ _ _ _ _ _ _ _ _ _ _ / _ _ _ _ _

Q12.

Embayed finitely

Clue: *Oasis debut*

_ _ _ _ _ _ _ _ _ / _ _ _ _ _

Q13.

Cow hotrod

Clue: *This person's nemesis can't climb stairs*

_ _ _ _ _ _ / _ _ _

Q14.
Flowery twats

Clue: *Ramshackle Torquay accommodation*

_ _ _ _ _ _ / _ _ _ _ _ _

Q15.
Ellen zipped

Clue: *There's a whole lotta love for this British band*

_ _ _ / _ _ _ _ _ _ _ _

Q16.
Rugby talons

Clue: *Home of the Pyramid Stage*

_ _ _ _ _ _ _ _ _ _

Q17.
Heed Gogh

Clue: *You might find one in your garden*

_ _ _ _ _ _ _ _

Q18.
Bullfight feral snakes

Clue: *Some pubs serve this meal all day*

_ _ _ _ / _ _ _ _ _ _ _ / _ _ _ _ _ _ _ _

Q19.
Downhill wettish wine

Clue: *Mr Toad and the gang*

_ _ _ / _ _ _ _ / _ _ / _ _ _ / _ _ _ _ _ _ _

Q20.
Cello sorry

Clue: *A luxury drive*

_ _ _ _ _ / _ _ _ _ _

Q21.
Cash find hips

Clue: *Sprinkle with salt and vinegar*

_ _ _ _ / _ _ _ / _ _ _ _ _

Q22.
Advent bird

Clue: *Hapless office boss*

_ _ _ _ _ / _ _ _ _ _

Q23.

Boats reef

Clue: *Eaten on Sunday*

_ _ _ _ _ / _ _ _ _

Q24.

Trashier yoke

Clue: *Ee bah gum that's a proper brew*

_ _ _ _ _ _ _ _ _ / _ _ _

Q25.

Looney Ned

Clue: *Optical attraction in the capital*

_ _ _ _ _ _ / _ _ _

Q26.
Mayor Lila

Clue: *Brings you letters*

_ _ _ _ _ / _ _ _ _

Q27.
Demonic cycling tarts

Clue: *Celebrities do the Charleston*

_ _ _ _ _ _ _ _ / _ _ _ _ / _ _ _ _ _ _ _

Q28.
Cajun oink

Clue: *Fly the red, white and blue*

_ _ _ _ _ / _ _ _ _

Q29.
Bye old

Clue: *Peckham's famous trader*

_ _ _ / _ _ _

Q30.
Meat rodent

Clue: *View up-to-date artworks*

_ _ _ _ / _ _ _ _ _ _

BOND FILMS

Your mission, reader, is to find the ten 007 films hidden in this puzzle. Good luck.

```
U  P  D  M  N  J  Y  V  O  Y  R  M  O  L  T
E  I  D  K  R  D  A  G  Z  N  K  C  W  I  H
P  L  M  G  O  L  D  F  I  N  G  E  R  C  U
P  R  A  B  A  L  R  T  A  A  H  Y  Q  E  N
M  N  E  Y  O  R  E  I  E  H  F  S  E  N  D
J  N  G  K  O  R  H  E  C  J  T  S  II C  E
R  N  J  O  A  R  T  E  N  T  Z  U  Y  E  R
D  J  N  K  Y  R  O  G  B  U  L  P  E  T  B
K  R  D  G  E  L  N  N  S  D  M  O  C  O  A
D  T  H  H  R  D  A  O  I  M  J  T  U  K  L
B  H  E  S  O  F  E  C  O  S  T  C  V  I  L
Y  N  I  E  R  A  I  H  O  M  A  O  E  L  C
Q  V  Q  H  Z  N  D  G  Q  E  S  C  X  L  F
S  K  Y  F  A  L  L  R  E  T  O  N  W  I  K
E  I  D  T  E  L  D  N  A  E  V  I  L  M  F
```

Casino Royale   Licence To Kill   Skyfall
Die Another Day   Live and Let Die   Thunderball
Dr No   Moonraker
Goldfinger   Octopussy

AWKWARD TV MOMENTS

Relive these British telly moments that made the nation awkwardly chuckle and/or cringe itself inside out.

ACROSS

2. First name of the nasty contestant chucked out of the first ever UK *Big Brother* (4)

5. Tripped on their cape at the 2015 Brit awards (7)

6. First name of judge who accidentally said 'bollocks' on *Strictly Come Dancing* (5)

8. Suffered a wardrobe malfunction at the 2001 National Television Awards. Richard is her husband. (4)

9. Awkward singers sing awkwardly, and then Britain gets *nul points* (10)

10. Surname of British comedian whose *Great British Bake Off* flapjacks become a meme (7)

DOWN

1. *Come Dine With Me*'s most famous moment. What a sad little life, _ _ _ _. (4)

3. Pick the wrong consonants and vowels and you could spell out something to make you blush (9)

4. Baby elephant poos all over the floor on this show in the 1960s (4, 5)

7. Absolutely lost it at the 'judges' house' stage of *X Factor*. Went on to become a popular presenter. (5)

NO BRITISH PLEASE!

Here's one for all you geography buffs. Let's take a trip around the world for a bunch of questions that have nothing to do with Britain at all (thought you'd like a break from Blighty).

Q1.
Ananas is the French word for which fruit?

Q2.
What is Japan's largest city?

Q3.
According to the Katie Melua song, how many bicycles are there in Beijing?

Q4.
How many countries share a border with Belgium?

Q5.
The Sound of Music, Sigmund Freud and the house of Habsburg are all linked to which country?

Q6.
Which country's Grand Prix race takes place on the Marina Bay Street Circuit?

Q7.
What is the capital of Mexico?

Q8.
In which city would you find St Basil's Cathedral, known for its colourful, onion-shaped domes?

Q9.
True or false: Antarctica is larger than Australia.

Q10.
True or false: The Arctic doesn't have any penguins.

Q11.
True or false: The Democratic Republic of Congo is the largest African country by area.

Q12.
Name the film, and coincidentally the place it's based in, from this quote: 'Of all the gin joints in all the towns in all the world, she walks into mine.'

Q13.
The Taj Mahal is in which Indian city?

Q14.
What is the largest country by both area and population in South America?

Q15.
Which of the major planets in our solar system is the most distant from the Sun?

Q16.

What is the national anthem of Belize?

Q17.

In which country would you find the city of Busan?

Q18.

How many cars are there in America?

Q19.

Where is considered to be the brightest spot on Earth?

Q20.

Which country's flag has three equally sized vertical stripes in this order: red, yellow, blue?

Q21.

Apia is the capital city of which Polynesian country?

Q22.

Who won the World Cup in 1998?

Q23.

In which German city would you find the Reichstag Building and the Brandenburg Gate?

Q24.

Where is the Frietmuseum, dedicated completely to chips?

Q25.

In which city would you find the railway terminal Penn Station?

Q26.

In which city is Elvis buried?

Q27.

Name four countries that have four-letter names.

Q28.
Nuuk is the capital city of which country?

Q29.
Which city has been formerly known as Byzantium and Constantinople?

Q30.
Which is the best country in the world?

CLASSIC BRITISH PRESENTS

Here you'll find ten things Brits love giving and receiving at Christmas and on birthdays. See if you can spot the red herring.

```
J  I  F  Z  Z  T  P  C  S  W  S  N  T  R  D
O  D  J  Y  H  E  H  K  Q  K  N  O  E  E  R
X  J  A  Y  R  W  O  H  C  V  F  V  E  D  A
J  W  V  F  I  O  X  O  H  Q  E  E  R  H  C
Y  X  U  T  B  I  S  J  X  W  J  L  T  E  A
D  M  Y  Z  M  Y  Z  V  F  S  O  T  S  R  N
E  X  I  D  N  E  Z  K  W  X  O  Y  Y  R  I
W  U  P  N  A  N  Z  O  M  W  R  J  T  I  R
Q  N  U  D  R  K  U  O  T  B  R  U  I  N  E
D  F  J  H  U  I  N  B  O  R  M  M  L  G  N
L  Q  F  B  K  K  L  K  J  B  M  P  A  K  N
A  O  O  I  S  G  W  O  D  S  M  E  U  O  E
S  D  H  D  V  B  D  O  E  K  W  R  Q  G  T
Q  E  D  C  T  Z  E  C  E  I  D  K  F  X  T
U  N  C  Q  L  Y  N  X  G  I  F  T  S  E  T
```

Booze   Novelty jumper   Red herring
Cookbook   Perfume   Tenner in a card
Funny socks   Quality Street
Lynx giftset   Quiz books

CHRISTMAS

Seeing as we finish the year with Christmas and seeing as a lot of you will be getting this book as a stocking filler (lucky you!), there's no more appropriate topic upon which to finish. Ho ho ho and all that.

Q1.
Which Brit sang the 1973 hit 'Step into Christmas'?

Q2.
When does Christmas start in Britain?

Q3.
According to a 2021 Very British Problems (@SoVeryBritish) Twitter poll, do the majority of Brits even like mince pies? Yes or no?

Q4.

In the 1996 Christmas special of *Only Fools and Horses*, 'Time on our Hands', what did Del and Rodney sell to finally become millionaires?

a) Bracelet
b) Watch
c) Diamond ring

Q5.

In earlier drafts of Charles Dickens' *A Christmas Carol*, which character was originally called 'Little Fred'?

Q6.

True or false: According to the Met Office, snowflakes have fallen in the UK on Christmas Day only twice (as of 2022) in the last fifty-two years?

Q7.

According to a Very British Problems (@SoVeryBritish) poll, should Yorkshire puddings be a part of Christmas dinner? Yes or no?

Q8.
On what date is St Stephen's Day?

Q9.
In Italy there's a dessert called *zuppa inglese*, translated as 'English soup'. What Christmassy British dessert is it suspected to be derived from?

Q10.
Which department store's Christmas advert in 2012 featured a snowman trying to obtain the perfect present for Mrs Snowman? It featured a cover version of Frankie Goes to Hollywood's classic song 'The Power of Love'.

Q11.
Which destructive pink and yellow character nabbed the Christmas number 1 spot in 1993?

Q12.
Which 2003 British Christmas film features the characters Billy Mack, Juliet, Natalie and the Prime Minister?

Q13.

Three of Father Christmas' reindeer have names that begin with D. Have a point for each you can name.

Q14.

In what year did Sir Cliff Richard release the chart-topping Christmas song, 'Mistletoe and Wine'?

    a)   1978
    b)   1988
    c)   1998

Q15.

Which of these acts has NOT had a Christmas number 1?

    a)   Girls Aloud
    b)   Matt Cardle
    c)   The Darkness

Q16.

Which historical figure banned Christmas festivities in 1647, after the English Civil War? The ban was lifted in 1660.

Q17.

In the song 'The Twelve Days of Christmas', how many geese are a-laying?

Q18.

What time is the Queen's Speech usually broadcast on television?

Q19.

In a tub of Quality Street, the toffee penny is covered with what colour wrapping?

Q20.

'Africa' is the scent of which deodorant brand, which has become a Christmas present staple?

Q21.

The world's longest what was made in Chesham, Buckinghamshire, in 2001?

    a)   Christmas cracker
    b)   Artificial Christmas tree
    c)   Yule log

Q22.

What should never be discussed at Christmas dinner, unless you want to spoil the day?

a) Politics/Brexit
b) Vaccines
c) Sex

Q23.

Michael Bublé, the man who croons Christmas hits out of everyone's stereo throughout December, is British. True or false?

Q24.

What might you pour alcohol over and set alight at the Christmas dinner table?

Q25.

According to the song title, what type of Christmastime does Paul McCartney have?

a) A Splendid Christmastime
b) A Wonderful Christmastime
c) A Decent Christmastime

Q26.

In 'Merry Christmas Mr Bean', what did the eponymous character get stuck on his head?

- a) A cracker hat
- b) A Christmas tree angel decoration
- c) A turkey

Q27.

What should you do if you're losing at Monopoly?

Q28.

Which fruit is traditionally left in a Christmas stocking?

Q29.

Who owns the fastest vehicle ever made?

Q30.

What is the true meaning of Christmas (according to me)?

- a) Goodwill to all men and women
- b) Being grateful for friends, family and good health
- c) The giving and receiving of new socks

ANSWERS

Weather (page 3)

Q1: a, It's Cornwall with 7.4 days of snow or sleet a year according to the Met Office.

Q2: b, A cloud

Q3: c, Scotland (Aberdeenshire)

Q4: c, -27.2°C

Q5: a, Rain

Q6: c, An umbrella

Q7: a, Storms

Q8: b, Summer (41 per cent of the vote share)

Q9: c, Umbrellas (maybe one of them belongs to Mary Poppins?)

Q10: b, Cardiff

Q11: a, Snow – 'I'm really snowed under here!'

Q12: c, 1963, in January

Q13: a, Rain

Q14: b, April, though January is actually wetter

Q15: c, Too much snow

Q16: a, Stratocumulus – a low layer of cloud with a clumpy base

Q17: b, 2020 (if you get it wrong it shows how much we *really* pay attention)

Q18: Could be all three, a point for each. If you said 'all three' have an extra point.

Q19: b, Michael Fish

Q20: b, He said a hurricane definitely wasn't on the way

Q21: c, Leaves. There's even a National Rail leaf timetable in autumn!

Q22: a, Wet Wet Wet

Q23: b, Wind speed

Q24: a, 1.65 metres

Q25: c, You can use any word or phrase (existing or made up) to describe rainfall, i.e. 'chucking it down', 'smashing it down', 'bucketing down', 'pissing it down' . . . depending on your mood/ wetness.

Q26: b, An egg, and you never can, it just creates a slightly warmer raw egg

Q27: b, Snoring
Q28: c, Thunder
Q29: c, Scottish
Q30: b, Duffel coat
Q31: c, 1952

Weather Defenders (page 14)

```
W H B G C S E S S A L G N U S
C S S S Z H F H U K O N I Y R
V J P O E B L A A Z A O R K E
W Q U A T E O R T G S Y E Y P
B X Y Z P N O L I R N C I T P
F A U R N I D E W E I A Z I
Z M L J A J R K P Q T T K R L
F O G A H A Z A C H T Q N U F
T Z M R C K L A F A I U P K S
S J T I W L K Q X O M E Y N S
S D T Y E V A H U U A X A I Q
B I D R Y X F V J W U Q L W N
Y O B N T M M A A J K B Q B B
E M W E L L I E S I E S E I Z
U U K B T O O M Q P S J G W A
```

Cockney Rhyming Slang (page 15)

Q1: c, Stairs – nice easy one to start you off
Q2: a, Noise
Q3: a, Port (the alcoholic drink)
Q4: b, Flowers – you have to get up early to sell them!
Q5: c, Hide – or 'skive'
Q6: a, Advice, which can prove to be cold comfort for some
Q7: b, Rain – pleasure for the garden, pain for the joints
Q8: c, A tale – and a sorry one at that; used to reference 'a beggar's tale'
Q9: a, Suit, often shortened to just 'whistle'
Q10: b, Sweetheart – did you get it right, me old treacle?
Q11: a, Curry
Q12: c, A watch – derived from fob watches
Q13: b, Hair – look at the state of your barnet!

Q14: a, Telly

Q15: a, Egg – a reference to food rationing

Q16: c, Suitcase – an item easily stolen in busy railway stations

Q17: b, Toast

Q18: c, Dice – like rats and mice, they can be found rolling around the floor

Q19: a, Believe – would you Adam and Eve it?

Q20: a, Alone – or 'all on my own'

Q21: c, Trouble – I'm in a spot of Barney Rubble

Q22: b, Face – give the nearest boat race a kiss (unless it would cause Barney Rubble)

Q23: c, Teeth

Q24: a, Thief

Q25: c, Clue

Q26: a, Piano – give us a tune on the Joanna, mate

Q27: c, Look – as in, 'have a butcher's at that!'

Q28: b, Socks – for some reason

Q29: b, Boozer (i.e. the pub!)

Q30: c, Money

Food and Drink (page 23)

Q1: a, Coronation Chicken, created for Elizabeth II's coronation in 1953

Q2: Red/ketchup (61 per cent of the vote share)

Q3: February, since 2007

Q4: c, Eat it yourself, obviously

Q5: b, Advocaat

Q6: b, Humbug

Q7: c, Beef, taking 39 per cent of the vote share, followed closely by chicken (33), then lamb (19) and finally pork (9)

Q8: b, 60.2 billion

Q9: c, PG Tips

Q10: Depends entirely on who's cooking them

Q11: a, McDonald's

Q12: b, *The Naked Chef*

Q13: b, Hot Chocolate, and the song would hit the Top 10 in multiple subsequent decades

Q14: c, Cheese & Onion

Q15: a, Sausages

Q16: c, Summer solstice

Q17: a, Marmalade

Q18: a, Browns Instantly, Seasons and Thickens in One

Q19: King Edward VII in 1902

Q20: b, Monmouthshire

Q21: b, Semi-skimmed, by quite a margin. Stay middling, Britain.

Q22: c, KitKat

Q23: The Red Lion (closely followed by The Crown and then The Royal Oak)

Q24: Peach

Q25: a, Pudding Lane

Q26: a, Pineapple

Q27: I'll leave you to argue amongst yourselves.

Q28: It's a name for a bread roll. As is bap. Or bun. Or cob. Or a million other things Brits call a bread roll, depending on where they're from.

Q29: Haggis is led into the room by a bagpiper during the Scottish celebration

Q30: b, Maiden Lane

Roast Dinner (page 32)

```
M V E E Z U O C H L I K E O C
H V D S R Y V A R G P C J A F
V S V A Y S Q R E C U C U U Y
E I I Q N O L R O A V L Q O W
G I A D W I H O S A I Y R I O
A W Y V A A Y T V F S K X L L
N P G X U R N S L V S T H L K
O G R O L I E O Z H C W I Q V
P G B A M E W S I L I K Q E H
T E M M I E A R R D B S U M S
I N A V R I E Y W O P R M F A
O A L A F S Y C M V H H Z F K
N K R N G W D P A R S N I P S
P Y M E M D H B U W V A E Z E
S I L T J D Q H D F K W C C E
```

Piece of Cake (page 33)

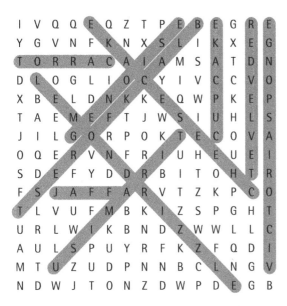

```
I  V  Q  Q  E  Q  Z  T  P  E  B  E  G  R  E
Y  G  V  N  F  K  N  X  S  L  I  K  X  E  G
T  O  R  R  A  C  A  I  A  M  S  A  T  D  N
D  L  O  G  L  I  O  C  Y  I  V  C  C  V  O
X  B  E  L  D  N  K  K  E  Q  W  P  K  E  P
T  A  E  M  E  F  T  J  W  S  I  U  H  L  S
J  I  L  G  O  R  P  O  K  T  E  C  O  V  A
O  Q  E  R  V  N  F  R  I  U  H  E  U  E  I
S  D  E  F  Y  D  D  R  B  I  T  O  H  T  R
F  S  J  A  F  F  A  R  V  T  Z  K  P  C  O
T  L  V  U  F  M  B  K  I  Z  S  P  G  H  T
U  R  L  W  I  K  B  N  D  Z  W  W  L  L  C
A  U  L  S  P  U  Y  R  F  K  Z  F  Q  D  I
M  T  U  Z  U  D  P  N  N  B  C  L  N  G  V
N  D  W  J  T  O  N  Z  D  W  P  D  E  G  B
```

British Events (page 34)

Q1: Bonfire Night, Guy Fawkes Night or Fireworks Night – all acceptable

Q2: It's St David's Day, a celebration for the patron saint of Wales, on 1 March

Q3: April Fools' Day, 1 April

Q4: June

Q5: The Notting Hill Carnival

Q6: Movember is in (drum roll) November!

Q7: Christmas Day, I'd say. Though, saying that, you might eat turkey every day. Or you might have goose or something weird on Christmas Day. Then again, you might not eat meat at all, you might be vegetarian, or even vegan! Which is fine. I don't want to upset anyone. In fact ... actually, I'll stop now.

Q8: Twenty-five million

Q9: Somerset

Q10: Pancakes, on Shrove Tuesday

Q11: Trooping the Colour

Q12: Double Gloucester

Q13: Plough Monday

Q14: Hocktide – a very old term used to signify the Monday and Tuesday in the second week after Easter
Q15: Trafalgar Square
Q16: Nettle
Q17: The first Monday in February
Q18: 2002
Q19: Three
Q20: False, it was formerly known as the Great Spring Show
Q21: At Crufts, hopefully
Q22: Easter egg, in 1873
Q23: August
Q24: Your 100th birthday. Unless Prince William is reading this, then the correct answer is hopefully 'all of them so far'.
Q25: Cambridgeshire
Q26: Goose
Q27: April
Q28: The River Thames. This annual ceremony sees 'swan uppers' rounding up, catching, ringing then releasing mute swans along the river.
Q29: November
Q30: It's the second one, and I bet you feel silly after reading out both of those

Very British Music Festivals (page 41)

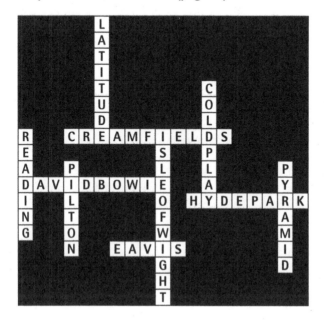

British Bands (page 42)

British Sports (page 43)

Q1: Cambridge, with 85 wins to Oxford's 80
Q2: A dead heat
Q3: The London Marathon
Q4: The Queen
Q5: Bog snorkelling, held annually in Llanwrtyd Wells
Q6: Scotland and England, in 1872
Q7: The US Open
Q8: Peterborough United
Q9: Horses, at Burghley Horse Trials
Q10: Canada
Q11: Sir Stanley Matthews
Q12: 'Super' Saturday
Q13: Roger Bannister, in 1954
Q14: James Anderson
Q15: Alexandra Palace in north London
Q16: Alun Wyn Jones
Q17: Quidditch
Q18: 20
Q19: Motorcycles

Q20: True, he exuded typical British politeness
Q21: Brian Clough
Q22: Extreme Ironing
Q23: 2002
Q24: Everton
Q25: 54
Q26: 22
Q27: c, 41
Q28: Red Rum
Q29: Sir Henry Cooper
Q30: Edinburgh
Q31: A bicycle

Who Said It? (page 50)

Quote: 'It is a well-known fact that ninety per cent of all foreign tourists come from abroad.'
Answer: Del Boy

Quote: 'Now this is not the end. It is not even the beginning of the end. But it is, perhaps, the end of the beginning.'
Answer: Winston Churchill

Quote: 'Reality leaves a lot to the imagination.'
Answer: John Lennon

Quote: 'Jogging is for people who aren't intelligent enough to watch television.'
Answer: Victoria Wood

Quote: 'Let us not take ourselves too seriously. None of us has a monopoly on wisdom.'
Answer: Queen Elizabeth II

Prime Ministers (page 52)

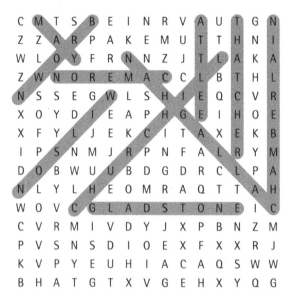

```
C M T S B E I N R V A U T G N
Z Z A R P A K E M U T T H N I
W L O Y F R N N Z J T L A K A
Z W N O R E M A C C L B T H L
N S S E G W L S H I E Q C V R
X O Y D I E A P H G E I H O E
X F Y L J E K C I T A X E K B
I P S N M J R P N F A L R Y M
D O B W U U B D G D R C L P A
N L Y L H E O M R A Q T T A H
W O V C G L A D S T O N E I C
C V R M I V D Y J X P B N Z M
P V S N S D I O E X F X X R J
K V P Y E U H I A C A Q S W W
B H A T G T X V G E H X Y Q G
```

Strange Historical Happenings (page 53)

Q1: True

Q2: False, it's a place in New Zealand with eighty-five letters, called (deep breath) Taumatawhakatangihangakoauauotamateaturi pukakapikimaungahoronukupokaiwhenuakitanatahu.
Well done if you were able to read out the question and the answer by the way.

Q3: True

Q4: False

Q5: True, he was concerned his soldiers were doing more golfing than archery practice

Q6: True

Q7: True, the scent was called 'Madeleine'

Q8: False, sadly

Q9: True

Q10: True

Q11: False, it was 500kg – half a tonne. Hope they got her a lot of crackers too.

Q12: True, apparently

Q13: False

Q14: True: light reflecting from the glass of the Walkie-Talkie building
(20 Fenchurch Street) on 29 August 2013, caused part of a parked
Jaguar to melt
Q15: True
Q16: False
Q17: True
Q18: False
Q19: True: erected around 3000BC, Stonehenge was already 500–1,000
years old before the first pyramid was built
Q20: False
Q21: False. If you said true, well, may you find the help you need.
Q22: False
Q23: True
Q24: False
Q25: False, it's nearly 6,000
Q26: False
Q27: False
Q28: True
Q29: False
Q30: True, weirdly

Daft British Place Names (page 60)
Q1: a, Crapstone in Devon
Q2: b, Scratchy Bottom in Dorset
Q3: a, Giggleswick in Yorkshire
Q4: a, Curry Mallet in Somerset
Q5: b, Barton in the Beans in Leicestershire
Q6: a, New Invention, in both Walsall and Shropshire
Q7: b, Dull in Perth and Kinross
Q8: a, Wetwang in Yorkshire
Q9: b, Catbrain in south Gloucestershire
Q10: b, Wham Bottom Lane in Rochdale
Q11: a, Thong in Kent
Q12: a, Lower Swell in Gloucestershire
Q13: a, Bitchfield in Lincolnshire
Q14: a, The River Piddle in Dorset
Q15: b, Fanny Barks in Durham
Q16: a, Wallyford in East Lothian
Q17: They're BOTH in Norfolk!
Q18: a, Titty Ho in Wellingborough
Q19: a, Booze in North Yorkshire
Q20: b, Barf House in North Yorkshire

Q21: a, Beer in Devon
Q22: a, Mumbles in Swansea
Q23: b, Godmanchester in Cambridgeshire
Q24: a, Witts End in Bedfordshire
Q25: a, Twatt in the Orkney Islands
Q26: b, Silly Lane in Lancaster
Q27: a, Ingle Pingle in Leicestershire
Q28: a, Ha-Ha Road in London
Q29: b, Inner Ting Tong in Devon
Q30: a, Peterborough

Where the Hell is that Museum?! (page 66)
The Fitzwilliam Museum – Cambridge
The National Railway Museum – York
The Victoria and Albert Museum – London
The Ashmolean Museum – Oxford
The Derwent Pencil Museum – Keswick
The Museum of Witchcraft and Magic – Cornwall
Big Pit National Coal Museum – Pontypool
British Lawnmower Museum – Southport, Merseyside
House of Marbles – Devon
Museum of Childhood – Edinburgh

The London Underground (page 68)
Q1: Vauxhall or Victoria
Q2: Escalator
Q3: The Metropolitan Line, opened in 1863
Q4: North, with 90 per cent of all stations. Greedy.
Q5: 2008
Q6: True; 55 per cent in fact
Q7: Green Park. It was renamed after reconstruction resulted in the closure of the entrance on Dover Street.
Q8: Red
Q9: Selfridges
Q10: 1930s (1931 to be precise)
Q11: The District Line with sixty stations
Q12: Jerry Springer
Q13: The bubonic plague
Q14: Heathrow
Q15: Acton Town
Q16: Woodside Park
Q17: Mansion House and South Ealing

Q18: Bank
Q19: Clapham Common
Q20: Marylebone
Q21: True
Q22: Walford East
Q23: 20.5mph
Q24: Covent Garden and Leicester Square – only 250 metres!
Q25: Burnt Oak
Q26: Oval
Q27: Ealing Broadway, Fulham Broadway or Tooting Broadway
Q28: Belsize Park
Q29: Arsenal
Q30: Battersea Power Station

How Old is the Building? (page 75)
Answers from oldest to youngest:

1. Stonehenge – From 3000BC to 2000BC
2. Hadrian's Wall – Begun 122
3. Westminster Abbey – Founded 960
4. Palace of Westminster (aka Houses of Parliament) – 1016
5. Tintern Abbey – 1131
6. The Globe Theatre – 1599
7. Chatsworth House – 1687–1708
8. Buckingham Palace – Built 1703–1705
9. Big Ben – Construction started 1843, opened 1859
10. The Royal Albert Hall – 1871
11. Blackpool Tower – 1891–1894
12. Original Wembley Stadium – 1923
13. Battersea Power Station – Construction begun 1929
14. The Severn Bridge – Opened 1966
15. The Tardis Police Box, Earl's Court – 1969
16. The Angel of the North – Constructed 1994–1998
17. London Eye – Opened 1999
18. The Eden Project – 2001
19. The Gherkin – Opened 2004
20. The Shard – Opened 2013

How to Speak British (page 76)
Q1: c
Q2: a (very rarely c, unless you're unusually calm/tranquillised; give yourself half a point if you went for this)

Q3:   b
Q4:   a
Q5:   c
Q6:   Could be any of them, to be honest, depending on your mood or how many cups of tea you've had. Give yourself a point, whatever you said.
Q7:   a, but sometimes c (which is also an extremely risky option). Most likely it's a.
Q8:   c. If you said a or b then get out now, this book won't be for you
Q9:   c
Q10: a or c, a point for either!
Q11: c, usually
Q12: b
Q13: c. Extra point if this question made you fetch a biscuit
Q14: All three. Gift yourself a custard cream for any answer!
Q15: c
Q16: a or b, depending on how you roll. Never c. Sorry for saying 'how you roll'. For more things slightly American, see page 90.
Q17: b
Q18: b
Q19: Yes
Q20: c
Q21: c
Q22: c
Q23: Not a
Q24: c
Q25: c
Q26: b
Q27: Probably a, isn't it?
Q28: c
Q29: c
Q30: It's all three, really, isn't it? Such a joyous yet stressful time.
Q31: b
Q32: c, ring the GP
Q33: All three, depending on time of week and number of teenagers present
Q34: c
Q35: All three

America! (page 90)
Q1:   12 May. Though it should be 5 December, if you ask me.
Q2:   c, rather alarmingly
Q3:   b, A sandwich

Q4: b, Venti, which is about a pint of coffee. Ridiculous.
Q5: A new season
Q6: b. Crackers, isn't it?
Q7: Nowhere, hopefully, but have a point for 'round your waist or hips'
Q8: They'd change it to 'transportation'
Q9: Shopping cart, most likely
Q10: c, Eaterie
Q11: Vermont or Virginia
Q12: Two points if you said, 'there isn't one', no points if you said, 'I can't think of one'
Q13: s
Q14: b, The Super Bowl
Q15: Tombstone
Q16: The Happy Meal from McDonald's
Q17: South Dakota
Q18: b, A main course
Q19: Peanut butter and jam, though you probably said 'jelly' instead of jam, didn't you? Shame.
Q20: Abraham Lincoln
Q21: Gray
Q22: a, A submarine sandwich. A cigar is a 'stogie' and c is a red herring.
Q23: c, Harley-Davidson
Q24: The Fonz, in a 1977 episode of *Happy Days*
Q25: b, Cheers (also the name of the show it featured in)
Q26: b, Let's postpone discussion about it for now
Q27: Donald Trump. He later deleted the tweet but also implied the wording was intentional.
Q28: False, they're just agreeing with you
Q29: b, Cookies
Q30: They think it sounds French and therefore 'proper'

All Creatures Great and British (page 98)
Q1: He's a cat. And he's pink.
Q2: c, Corgi
Q3: A parrot. An extra point if you noted it was the fictional 'Norwegian Blue' variety.
Q4: Scottish Deerhound or Scottish Terrier
Q5: a, English Lop
Q6: The toad
Q7: Second! Pipped to the number one spot by Germany.
Q8: Pharaoh, Isis and Teo
Q9: Larry the Cat

Q10: Pigs

Q11: Bagpuss, of the much-loved British children's series which aired in 1974

Q12: Bear

Q13: c, A delicious plump-breasted pigeon

Q14: Leicester City

Q15: c, Papillon, a small toy spaniel

Q16: The Wombles, originally appearing in a series of children's novels in 1968, going on to receive national fame in the 1970s in the BBC-commissioned television show

Q17: b, Paul McCartney's dog

Q18: On the Welsh flag

Q19: False, though there are around eleven million pet cats! (sixty-seven million people)

Q20: b, E. H. Shepard

Q21: a, Guide dogs

Q22: A badger

Q23: Emu

Q24: c, Rattlesnake

Q25: Jaguar

Q26: A nightingale

Q27: False, it's called a Jenny

Q28: c, Chinook. It's a dog breed.

Q29: b, A clowder

Q30: Hedwig

British Tree or Bird? (page 106)

Trees:
European Larch
Hornbeam
Rowan
Spindle
Whitebeam

Birds:
Avocet
Brambling
Linnet
Nuthatch
Redpoll

Brits on Holiday (page 108)

Q1: Out of office
Q2: Skegness
Q3: Ryanair
Q4: Spain
Q5: Switzerland
Q6: False, it's Heathrow, which transports twice the number of travellers as second-placed Gatwick
Q7: b, $450,000. Bit pricey.
Q8: 28 and counting
Q9: [loud voice] 'DOES IT COME WITH CHIPS SIL VOOS PLATE MONSURE?'
Q10: Blackpool
Q11: A stick of rock
Q12: The London Eye
Q13: The Lake District National Park
Q14: Also midday
Q15: b, Malia
Q16: Scotland
Q17: Heinz Baked Beans
Q18: 603 miles
Q19: Wiltshire
Q20: Tate Modern
Q21: Brighton
Q22: Cups of tea
Q23: Ten years
Q24: No
Q25: *Wish You Were Here*
Q26: The Shard, at 309.6 metres
Q27: Benidorm
Q28: You can stand there all you like, your bag's in another country. (In all seriousness, the average wait time is said to be between 15 and 45 minutes.)
Q29: *A Place in the Sun*

Seaside Must-haves (page 115)

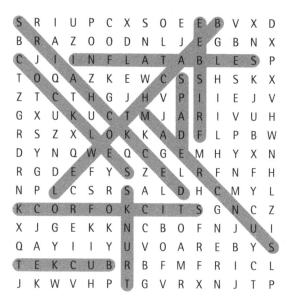

Petrol Station or Cheese? (page 116)

These five are cheeses:
Dovedale
Duddleswell
Hereford Hop
Swaledale
Y Fenni

These five are petrol stations:
Birchanger Green
Charnock Richard
Chieveley
Leigh Delamare
Michaelwood

Discovery and Invention (page 118)
Q1: a, Text message, sent by 22-year-old British software engineer Neil Papworth
Q2: c, The lava lamp

Q3: Tim Berners-Lee, in 1989
Q4: Cats' eyes
Q5: True. It was introduced in 1937.
Q6: University of Cambridge
Q7: Michael
Q8: b, Marks & Spencer
Q9: The British Museum, with a permanent collection of eight million works over ninety-four galleries
Q10: True, the i-LIMB was invented by David Gow in Edinburgh and launched in 2007
Q11: a, Benedict Cumberbatch
Q12: a, Clive Sinclair
Q13: Livingstone – the famous Victorian physician and explorer
Q14: James Dyson
Q15: Barclays
Q16: Quorn
Q17: Dolly
Q18: The Clifton Suspension Bridge in Bristol
Q19: b, Cricket
Q20: c, Beer
Q21: The lawnmower
Q22: False
Q23: c, Kettle
Q24: Edward Jenner (1749–1823)
Q25: a, Thomas Crapper
Q26: Toothbrushes
Q27: True, the British got there before the French with the Halifax Gibbet in the sixteenth century
Q28: c, Sir Walter Raleigh (1552–1618)
Q29: Arsenic poisoning
Q30: Pot Noodle

British Books (page 126)
Q1: c, *Harry Potter and the Chamber of Secrets*
Q2: *The Hobbit*
Q3: b, 1616
Q4: *Wuthering Heights*
Q5: The Booker Prize
Q6: Dawn French
Q7: 13¾
Q8: Verona
Q9: Gonzo

Q10: c, *Big Brother Goes Camping*
Q11: True. He only says it in the later films.
Q12: Answer to the Ultimate Question of Life, the Universe and Everything. (Will accept 'Meaning of Life' or similar.)
Q13: Paddington Bear, in 1958
Q14: *Lover*
Q15: The dictionary
Q16: b, Waterstones
Q17: b, *The Remains of the Day* by Kazuo Ishiguro
Q18: c, Lighthouse (*To the Lighthouse*)
Q19: Oscar Wilde
Q20: c, Life
Q21: 14
Q22: E. M. Forster
Q23: c, Adrian
Q24: *Orange*
Q25: b, Fitzwilliam
Q26: *Casino Royale*
Q27: *A Tale of Two Cities*
Q28: It uses every letter in the alphabet
Q29: Augustus Gloop, Veruca Salt, Violet Beauregarde and Mike Teavee
Q30: a, *Demon Dentist*
Q31: Phileas Fogg

The Play's the Thing (page 134)
Shylock – The Merchant of Venice
Mercutio – Romeo and Juliet
Domitius Enobarbus – Antony and Cleopatra
Oberon – A Midsummer Night's Dream
Polonius – Hamlet
Desdemona – Othello
Prospero – The Tempest
Macduff – Macbeth
Cordelia – King Lear
Dogberry – Much Ado About Nothing

Very British Soap Opera Crossword (page 136)

Name the Biscuit! (page 137)

Q1: Custard cream
Q2: Bourbon
Q3: Hobnob
Q4: Jaffa Cake
Q5: Oreo
Q6: Jammie dodger
Q7: Nice biscuit
Q8: Shortbread
Q9: Digestive
Q10: Ginger nuts
Q11: Garibaldi
Q12: Rich tea
Q13: Chocolate finger
Q14: Party ring
Q15: Choco Leibniz
Q16: Biscotti
Q17: Club
Q18: Pink wafers
Q19: Viscount

Q20: Malted milk
Q21: Stroopwafel
Q22: Viennese whirl
Q23: Viennese sandwich
Q24: Fig roll
Q25: Wagon wheel
Q26: KitKat
Q27: Macarons
Q28: Lady fingers

Tea Time! (page 143)

P	N	Y	Q	O	P	G	O	W	O	C	L	K	E	T	Z
B	C	E	D	U	C	Z	N	O	B	X	I	S	I	H	O
C	X	R	E	Y	C	H	L	I	S	F	W	L	C	F	M
C	F	G	J	J	G	O	F	G	L	O	G	K	E	U	M
J	X	L	Z	P	N	P	Q	A	F	E	B	Z	D	A	X
U	P	R	Z	G	Y	K	Y	J	N	J	E	I	T	V	K
X	F	A	P	J	M	O	C	U	G	V	D	J	O	B	S
E	M	E	E	L	I	M	O	M	A	H	C	W	R	O	H
H	O	C	K	M	U	G	G	E	A	R	L	F	J	A	R
I	S	G	H	P	O	H	R	S	H	E	C	I	B	B	D
M	W	J	U	Y	Q	A	S	E	D	N	U	Y	B	D	H
Y	E	D	J	C	G	A	Q	R	E	A	Z	M	O	M	S
G	Y	A	U	S	M	C	O	D	J	N	F	O	W	E	Y
E	N	G	L	I	S	H	B	R	E	A	K	F	A	S	T
C	C	N	O	G	T	N	I	M	R	E	P	P	E	P	Z

British Brands (page 144)
Q1: Mr Kipling
Q2: Marmite
Q3: Andrex
Q4: Pedigree Chum
Q5: Shredded Wheat
Q6: Thomas Cook it
Q7: British Airways
Q8: Peperami
Q9: Argos

Q10: Ambrosia Custard
Q11: Yorkshire Tea
Q12: BT
Q13: Cadbury's Creme Egg
Q14: Ronseal
Q15: Tesco
Q16: Domestos
Q17: Irn Bru
Q18: Polo (the mints, obviously, not the clothes with the little horse)
Q19: Aston Martin
Q20: Skittles
Q21: Penguin
Q22: John Lewis
Q23: Fry's Turkish Delight
Q24: Mr Muscle
Q25: Compare the Market
Q26: Cravendale
Q27: *Radio Times*
Q28: Sainsbury's
Q29: SodaStream
Q30: Bisto

British Shops (page 149)

V	Q	N	Q	B	G	P	W	S	T	H	Y	O	D	Z
I	E	L	O	H	H	A	M	E	W	Z	W	N	J	P
H	I	O	K	L	I	W	K	L	P	L	A	N	J	F
T	T	V	K	T	R	S	N	F	X	L	X	W	M	A
S	H	M	R	Q	B	Y	V	R	S	T	X	P	X	N
F	M	O	H	W	P	T	T	I	S	G	D	M	U	U
N	S	S	I	Y	C	R	R	D	W	A	O	D	D	H
E	R	Q	I	S	I	E	A	G	M	T	U	V	Y	Y
F	P	B	F	W	V	B	I	E	J	U	B	G	P	N
B	A	F	O	I	E	I	V	S	P	G	T	Z	H	E
H	A	P	R	X	W	L	C	A	H	I	J	T	U	E
M	R	W	P	S	A	I	N	S	B	U	R	Y	S	S
S	G	Y	Q	F	M	L	T	H	W	D	L	T	V	D
K	O	R	E	S	A	R	F	F	O	E	S	U	O	H
K	S	X	S	T	H	Z	X	W	A	J	H	J	V	Q

British Counties (page 150)

Q1: c, 48
Q2: c, 33
Q3: Rutland
Q4: Merseyside
Q5: Lincolnshire
Q6: Neath Port Talbot or Newport
Q7: Kent
Q8: North Yorkshire
Q9: City of London
Q10: Cornwall
Q11: Inverness-shire
Q12: Derbyshire
Q13: Cambridgeshire
Q14: Tyne and Wear
Q15: Three – West Midlands, West Sussex and West Yorkshire
Q16: Worcestershire
Q17: None
Q18: Berkshire
Q19: Lancashire
Q20: Norfolk
Q21: Dorset
Q22: Shropshire
Q23: You could have had Gloucestershire, Oxfordshire, Wiltshire, Somerset, Worcestershire and Warwickshire
Q24: Daniel Craig
Q25: Nottinghamshire
Q26: Leicestershire
Q27: Hertfordshire
Q28: Hampshire
Q29: Oxfordshire
Q30: Bedfordshire
Q31: Isle of Wight
Q32: Northumberland
Q33: Cumbria

British County or American State? (page 156)

1. County: Norfolk
2. County: Cornwall
3. State: Florida
4. County: Lincolnshire
5. State: Texas

6. State: Iowa
7. County: North Yorkshire
8. State: California
9. State: Nevada
10. County: Berkshire

Very British Conundrums (page 158)

Q1: Cucumber sandwiches
Q2: Spice Girls
Q3: Manchester United
Q4: *EastEnders*
Q5: Bin day
Q6: Winston Churchill
Q7: Sticky toffee pudding
Q8: Big Ben
Q9: Isaac Newton
Q10: Charlie Chaplin
Q11: Westminster Abbey
Q12: *Definitely Maybe*
Q13: *Doctor Who*
Q14: *Fawlty Towers*
Q15: Led Zeppelin
Q16: Glastonbury
Q17: Hedgehog
Q18: Full English breakfast
Q19: *The Wind in the Willows*
Q20: Rolls-Royce
Q21: Fish and chips
Q22: David Brent
Q23: Roast beef
Q24: Yorkshire Tea
Q25: London Eye
Q26: Royal Mail
Q27: *Strictly Come Dancing*
Q28: Union Jack
Q29: Del Boy
Q30: Tate Modern

Bond Films (page 169)

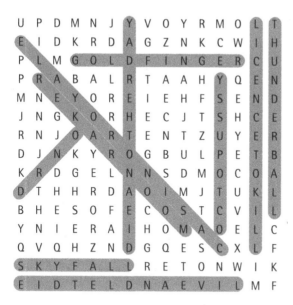

Awkward TV Moments (page 170)

No British Please! (page 171)

Q1: Pineapple
Q2: Tokyo
Q3: Nine million
Q4: Four: France, Germany, Luxembourg and the Netherlands
Q5: Austria
Q6: Singapore
Q7: Mexico City
Q8: Moscow
Q9: True. It's roughly twice the size. It's larger than Europe too.
Q10: True
Q11: False, it's Algeria. The DR of Congo is second.
Q12: Casablanca
Q13: Agra
Q14: Brazil
Q15: Neptune
Q16: God Save The Queen
Q17: South Korea
Q18: Bloody loads! Nearly 300 million registered ones, anyway.
Q19: The Vegas Strip, as measured by NASA
Q20: Romania
Q21: Samoa
Q22: France
Q23: Berlin
Q24: Belgium
Q25: New York City
Q26: He's still alive. Or Memphis.
Q27: Your choices were Chad, Cuba, Fiji, Iran, Iraq, Laos, Mali, Niue, Oman, Peru and Togo
Q28: Greenland
Q29: Istanbul
Q30: Correct!

Classic British Presents (page 177)

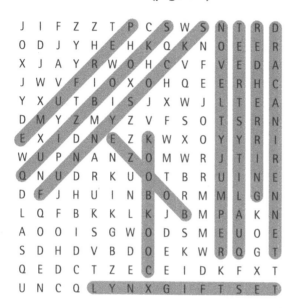

```
J  I  F  Z  Z  T  P  C  S  W  S  N  T  R  D
O  D  J  Y  H  E  H  K  Q  K  N  O  E  E  R
X  J  A  Y  R  W  O  H  C  V  F  V  E  D  A
J  W  V  F  I  O  X  O  H  Q  E  E  R  H  C
Y  X  U  T  B  I  S  J  X  W  J  L  T  E  A
D  M  Y  Z  M  Y  Z  V  F  S  O  T  S  R  N
E  X  I  D  N  E  Z  K  W  X  O  Y  Y  R  I
W  U  P  N  A  N  Z  O  M  W  R  J  T  I  R
O  N  U  D  R  K  U  O  T  B  R  U  I  N  E
D  F  J  H  U  I  N  B  O  R  M  M  L  G  N
L  Q  F  B  K  K  L  K  J  B  M  P  A  K  N
A  O  O  I  S  G  W  O  D  S  M  E  U  O  E
S  D  H  D  V  B  D  O  E  K  W  R  Q  G  T
Q  E  D  C  T  Z  E  C  E  I  D  K  F  X  T
U  N  C  Q  L  Y  N  X  G  I  F  T  S  E  T
```

Christmas (page 178)

Q1:   Elton John
Q2:   Earlier every year
Q3:   Yes: 57 per cent, No 43 per cent (20,654 votes in total)
Q4:   b, Watch
Q5:   Tiny Tim
Q6:   False, it's happened 38 times
Q7:   Yes: 73 per cent, No: 27 per cent (16,576 votes in total)
Q8:   26 December
Q9:   Trifle
Q10: John Lewis
Q11: Mr Blobby
Q12: *Love Actually*
Q13: Dasher, Dancer and Donner
Q14: b, 1988
Q15: c, The Darkness
Q16: Oliver Cromwell
Q17: Six
Q18: 3pm
Q19: Gold

Q20: Lynx

Q21: a, Christmas cracker, at 63.1 metres long

Q22: All three. Steer well clear!

Q23: False, he's Canadian

Q24: I hope you said Christmas pudding and not 'Uncle John'

Q25: b, A Wonderful Christmastime

Q26: c, A turkey

Q27: Accidentally turn the board upside down and storm out

Q28: Have a point if you said any of the myriad types of orange or simply 'orange'

Q29: Father Christmas

Q30: c, The giving and receiving of new socks

ACKNOWLEDGEMENTS

Thank you to Juliet Mushens at Mushens Entertainment, and to Emily Barrett and Sarah Kennedy and all the team at Little, Brown. And thank you to Sean, who loved a quiz.

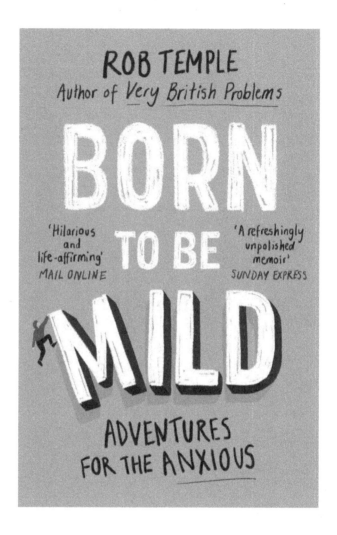

ROB TEMPLE
Author of *Very British Problems*

BORN TO BE

'Hilarious and life-affirming'
MAIL ONLINE

'A refreshingly unpolished memoir'
SUNDAY EXPRESS

TO BE

MILD

ADVENTURES FOR THE ANXIOUS

A funny, life-affirming memoir from the creator of Very British Problems, about how to start again when everything's gone wrong.